GHOST STORIES OF ARIZONA and NEW MEXICO

Dan Asfar

Lone Pine Publishing International

The Publisher: Lone Pine Publishing International
Distributed by Lone Pine Publishing
1808 B Street NW, Suite 140
Auburn, WA 98001
USA

Websites: www.lonepinepublishing.com
www.ghostbooks.net

National Library of Canada Cataloguing in Publication Data

Asfar, Dan, 1973-
Ghost stories of Arizona & New Mexico / Dan Asfar.

ISBN-13: 978-976-8200-15-0
ISBN-10: 976-8200-15-4

1. Ghosts--Arizona. 2. Ghosts--New Mexico. 3. Tales--Arizona. 4. Tales--New Mexico. I. Title.

GR110.A6A84 2006   398.2'09791'05   C2006-901451-5

Photo Credits: Every effort has been made to accurately credit photographers. Any errors or omissions should be directed to the publisher for changes in future editions. The photographs in this book are reproduced with the kind permission of the following sources: Cottonwood Hotel (p. 193); Anton Foltin (p. 4–5); Lise Gagne (p. 94); Library of Congress (p. 25: HABS ARIZ,2-TOMB,11-2; p. 28: HABS ARIZ,2-TOMB,18-2; p. 51: USZ62-104693; p. 60: HABS NM,4-CIM,7-2; p. 122: USZ62-103463; p. 198: USZ62-42905); Earl Owens (p. 101, p. 104); Rock Resorts (p. 80); Edward F. Rozylowicz (p. 39); Paul Senyszyn (p. 114); Dustin Stellar (p. 111); *The American West in the Nineteenth Century*, by John Grafton, Dover Publications, 1992 (p. 55, p. 65); Yuma Visitors Bureau (p. 45).

The stories, folklore and legends in this book are based on the author's collection of sources including individuals whose experiences have led them to believe they have encountered phenomena of some kind or another. They are meant to entertain, and neither the publisher nor the author claims these stories represent fact.

PC: P5

For Carmen and Brett and the Gringo Paradisio

Contents

Acknowledgments

Skeptics will roll their eyes at the mention of the nonfiction paranormal genre. Nonfiction paranormal? Surely an oxymoron. Nevertheless, whether or not one chooses to believe in them, every account in this volume is based on purported hauntings set in the American Southwest. Some are old folktales retold, while others are based on interviews with individuals claiming to have come face-to-face with phenomena beyond their understanding. Still others are rooted in tales that have been unearthed by other authors in this genre.

Allow me to begin, then, by acknowledging the invaluable contribution of those whose tales informed and inspired many of the stories in this book. First, thanks to the individuals who took the time to share their bizarre experiences. Because of the assumptions that are often made about people who claim to have seen ghosts, the identities of these witnesses have been protected and given pseudonyms where they appear in the text.

Writers whose research has been invaluable to this text include Jane Eppinga, author of *Arizona Twilight Tales: Good Ghosts, Evil Spirits & Blue Ladies*; the prolific Antonio Garcez, author of the series *Adobe Angels*, which forms an extensive record of supernatural activity in the region; and Father Henry, whose interview in *The Ghosts of Albuquerque* was the inspiration for "The Evil Under the Bed." Thanks to Michael Connelly for his telling of the Boy Scouts' supernatural canon in *Riders in the Sky: The Ghosts and Legends of Philmont Scout Ranch*. I must also acknowledge Ellen Robson's work, *Haunted Arizona: Ghosts of the Grand Canyon State*. This book owes much to your efforts.

Introduction

Phoenix, Albuquerque, Los Angeles, New York, Hong Kong, Dublin, London…really, it doesn't matter where you are. Whether we're talking about the American Southwest or the Greek Archipelago, there are sure to be ghosts. Or, perhaps more accurately, there are sure to be ghost stories. And there always have been.

Seriously. Go back. I mean all the way back. As far back as *The Iliad*, one of the original narratives of Western civilization. Before there was *Psycho* or *The Shining* or *The Ring*, there was Homer's epic poem in which the recently slain warrior, Patroclus, comes back from the dead to warn Achilles of his imminent death. This is just one document revealing early man's fascination with mortality.

While Chinese folklore has the spirits of long dead ancestors routinely rising from the grave, old European narratives also reveal a definite preoccupation with the denizens of the afterlife, from Count Vlad the Impaler, to Shakespeare's repeated use of ghosts in his plays, to Keats' "Belle Dame Sans Mercy." That's to say nothing of Victorian England's obsession with Spiritualism and the resulting gothic narratives that fueled the popular imagination. Edgar Allan Poe, Bram Stoker, H.P. Lovecraft and Stephen King are some of the more recognizable raconteurs who have spun supernatural stories over the years, as the genre grew to find expression in every storytelling medium—novels, comic books, films and video games.

The book you hold in your hands belongs to a peculiar genre called paranormal nonfiction. These are stories dealing with supernatural subject matter that are purported to be true, or, where a definitive narrative exists, *based* on events that a certain people believe to be true. Some of the following accounts read like straightforward fact-based reporting, based on interviews with witnesses who claim to have had paranormal experiences. As is often the case with such stories, all the witnesses have requested anonymity, and their wishes have been respected. Their experiences have been recounted in stories like "A Visitation in the Wilderness," "Not Just Another Apartment Suite," "The Thing That Happened at Bonito Lake" and "A Helpful Haunt in Phoenix."

These eyewitness accounts, however, only make up part of this book. The paranormal nonfiction canon also includes folklore—tales that have been told and retold over the years that usually say something about a region's culture, morals or history, *and*, it might be added, are believed by some people to be true. The Headless Horseman in New England, Resurrection Mary in Chicago and the Red Dwarf in Detroit are three famous examples of supernatural folklore. Arizona and New Mexico have their own, the legend of La Llorona easily being the most recognizable.

The very nature of these stories makes a certain amount of fictionalization necessary. While the folkloric feel is still there, retellings always vary according to the storyteller, and certain creative license is necessary when one endeavors to approach these stories. This will be made abundantly clear in stories such as "The Phantom Train of the Wilcox Playa" and "The Ghost of Tom Wright."

On a final note, all but four of the tales in this book take place exclusively in either Arizona or New Mexico. "Highway 666: What's in a Name?" has been included because though Highway 666 cuts through Utah and Colorado, one of its endpoints is in Gallup, New Mexico. "Betrayal in the Anza Borrego," "One More Tragedy in Vallecito" and "The Ghost of Poor Old Eilley Bowers" have been given a place because, though Vallecito and the Anza Borrego Desert are in southern California and Eilley Bowers suffered and died in Nevada, all three occupy prominent places in the folklore of the region. They are three ghost stories of the Southwest, and are included because they stand as interesting representations of the entire region.

But enough with the explanations. I have kept you for too long. It's time to turn the page, and delve into the ghostly lore of Arizona and New Mexico.

1

Ghosts of the Frontier

The Phantom Train of the Wilcox Playa

Fortune hunters were as common as tumbleweeds in 19th-century Arizona, so nobody would have missed Billy Barclay too much if he had met his end on the sun-baked expanse of the Wilcox Playa. Well, nobody besides Jenny Martin—the sole cause of young Barclay's foolhardy foray into the desert in the first place. It was gold that Billy was after, a mother lode of gold that was rumored to be located around Dos Cabezas in the deserts of the southeastern corner of Arizona. Normally, Billy would have been smarter than to take the whispered suppositions of mining speculators seriously, but the young man's smarts had been greatly compromised the day he laid eyes on Jenny Martin.

Until then, there had hardly been a more genteel, responsible, even-tempered resident of Tombstone, Arizona. Leaving his Iowa home behind him, Billy Barclay arrived at that most infamous Gomorrah of the American West in the 1870s. It was obvious from the moment his wagon pulled up that the young man was going to stand apart from the frontier rabble infesting the booming mining town. While the frontier settlement was populated by gamblers, gunfighters, prospectors, prostitutes and every other ne'er-do-well with an appreciation for mayhem, Billy Barclay himself was a picture of even-headed refinement.

Neither a miner, gambler, drinker nor gunfighter, Billy walked the dusty streets of Tombstone immune to the violence and desperation that surrounded him. In a town populated mainly by frantic young men all too willing to dig, claw or murder for a quick fortune, to be free of such desire made one a true eccentric. A placid-natured man in a town defined by a feverish need to strike it rich, Billy Barclay was most definitely an eccentric, staying away from all of the dubious activities that made Tombstone famous. Then Jenny Martin came to town, and for the first time in his life, Billy understood what it was to yearn for something.

She was his perfect match—just as moral, temperate and good-natured, with no appetite for the madness that afflicted the young town. Just as out of place there as Billy, she too was able to exist in that desperate settlement without needing any of the things that possessed the rest of the population. She too maintained a nearly freakish calm in one of the most frantic towns in the American West. Billy recognized all of this the instant he laid eyes on her, and he wanted to get to know her with a longing so intense that it frightened him. But even then, it was impossible for Billy to forget his personal conventions. He told himself that passion alone wasn't enough; a man hoping to court a woman of Jenny Martin's station required more than mere desire. A man would also need plenty of money. Therein lay the problem.

Though Barclay's serene disposition was good at keeping him out of trouble, it did nothing for his personal finances. One of the hardest truisms of the Old West stated that a man who didn't have the sand to risk too much wasn't likely to gain too much either. Was Billy Barclay modest and conservative? Yes. Was Billy Barclay an easygoing and moral gentleman? Sure. But was Billy Barclay a man of means? Hell no.

The sad fact was that Billy was about as poor as a starving coyote. Working odd jobs around Tombstone whenever opportunities arose, he had never once set foot in those smoke-filled saloons where fortune seekers stoked their personal ambitions, whispered rumors about hidden gold and silver and hatched harebrained schemes to get at it. He stayed clear of these men and their troubled affairs, and lived a peaceful life because of it. Peaceful and poor, that is. While other, more ambitious men were wandering out in the desert and returning back rich, Billy went day to day, risking nothing and gaining less—barely scraping by with the modest earnings he made fixing people's roofs, sweeping walkways and mopping floors. The truth was that he never felt as though he had reason to break his back for a buck. All it took was a smile from Jenny Martin, though, and Billy was transformed into the most desperate fortune hunter in town. There was no question in his mind; he needed to win Jenny Martin's hand. And for that, he would need money.

He overheard the rumor in one of town's watering holes while sitting beside two drunks—one young prospector, one old—who were whispering about a mother lode in the desert. Gold, the young man had said to his senior, lots of it, around Dos Cabezas. That was all the eager Billy Barclay needed to hear. He didn't waste another moment, rushing out of the saloon before he was able to hear the older prospector deliver his skeptical retort: "Hell, more rumors than cactus around these parts. A man'd have to be plumb loco to go out into that godforsaken desert on account of some damn rumor."

Plumb loco or just plain clueless. Barclay had never tried his hand at any kind of prospecting. He had no way of knowing that barroom rumors were often nothing more than wishful thinking said out loud, or that the desert between Tombstone and Dos Cabezas, a scorched expanse known as the Wilcox Playa, was littered with the bodies of those who had been seduced by similar optimistic musings. Jenny Martin was the only thing on his mind as he got his supplies together and loaded them up on his burro. And when it was time to plan his journey to Dos Cabezas, he was so optimistic that he decided on the most direct route—across the Wilcox Playa rather than around it. It was there, as Billy Barclay made his way across that barren plain, that the bizarre legend of the phantom train was born.

The trouble began on Billy's first night in the desert. The day's journey had been hot and difficult, but not enough to dampen the young man's spirits, and he was humming a happy tune to himself as he bedded down for the evening. Lost in his reveries over Jenny Martin, Billy made a hasty camp, oblivious to the fact that he hadn't picketed his burro down before going to sleep. Falling asleep with a grin on his face, the would-be prospector's sanguine outlook would not last the night.

It was still dark when he was jolted awake. He had no idea how much time had passed or what had broken his slumber, but his heart was pounding, his adrenaline was flowing, and the memory of a scream echoed in his head. Staring wide-eyed into the darkness, Billy was overcome with foreboding. He reached for his lantern with shaking hands, wondering if the scream he was sure he had just heard was the remnant of some nightmare, or if something was out there, lurking in the darkness.

The rasping screech was so close that he let out a startled shout. Billy recognized the sound instantly—it was a cougar, and a big one too, if he could make anything of its throaty growl rumbling in the blackness. All at once his thoughts turned to his burro. *What had happened to his donkey?* Seconds later there was a small flame in his lantern, and he looked just in time to catch sight of his nightmare—a massive four-legged shape loping away into the blackness. And there, lying on the blood-blackened ground mere yards away, was his burro, staring at him through lifeless eyes, still bleeding through the gaping wounds across its throat.

If Billy had had any kind of experience in the desert, at that point he might have questioned the fate of his expedition. Assuming he did find the fabled gold vein, without a pack animal to carry his supplies, he wouldn't be equipped to extract the precious metal from the earth. And even if he somehow did manage to mine the gold, there was no way he'd be able to carry it across the desert back to Tombstone. To make matters worse, he discovered that his water jug had been punctured, trampled by his burro during the cougar attack. The only water he had left was half a day's worth in his canteen.

Anyone who was thinking straight would probably have turned around, but then, except for thoughts of Jenny Martin, Billy could hardly be said to have been thinking at all. Even as he stood there looking down on the carcass of his burro illuminated by the fluttering light of his lantern, he was reminded of the day he caught sight of Jenny Martin unloading her father's pack on Allen Street. He smiled at the memory and, telling himself that no gold meant no Jenny, decided that he would load what supplies he could upon his back and continue on the next day. Determined as he was, nothing could change the fact that Billy was about as tender as a Tombstone tenderfoot could get, and resolve alone wasn't going to get him through the desolation of the Wilcox Playa.

"A man'd have to be plumb loco to go out into that godforsaken desert on account of some damn rumor."

It was a lesson that Billy learned the next day as the mid-day sun reached its zenith in the searing desert sky. Stumbling over the parched land, half his donkey's load piled atop his back, Billy began to wonder at the wisdom of his decision. He had drunk the last of his water that morning, and his throat was already aching for more. The bright and barren landscape offered no shelter from the relentless heat, and before long, it was all Billy could do to put one foot in front of the other.

Gone were the fanciful hopes of finding gold in the desert. Gone were the visions of Jenny Martin. All of Billy's thoughts were now bent on one thing—survival. He knew he would never last in the desert and needed to find a way back, but he no longer knew which way back *was*. The surrounding landscape all looked the same, and Billy began wondering if he was walking in circles. Shedding mining gear as the hours crawled by, the young would-be prospector had nothing on his back by the early afternoon. In a few more hours his breath was coming in dry, painful rasps and panic began to well up in his heart.

I'm not going to make it. At first it was just a thought, a single thought from the darkest place in his mind. Then it became a terrified realization—a mumbled mantra through dried and cracked lips. *I'm going to die. I'm going to die out here.*

He stumbled on a barrel cactus, collapsing and cutting it open with his knife to slake his thirst on its bitter juices. He took the pungent liquid as an affirmation. There was life in the desert; it was possible for things to live in the desert. Maybe he wasn't doomed. He took a deep breath. Stood up. Looked around.

He recalled what he had heard from Tombstone's more seasoned prospectors, that barrel cacti always leaned to the south. Taking note of the cactus before him, he headed out in the direction he imagined Tombstone would be. Now he forced a new thought. *I'm not going to die.* He said it out loud, and it calmed the panic in his veins. "I'm not going to die." Billy kept repeating it to himself and, for a short while, managed to convince himself that it might actually be true.

His optimism, however, came crashing down once again when he saw his dead burro, already rotting in the stifling heat; Billy realized that he'd spent the entire day walking in one big circle. He was back where he started, and he didn't even know where that was. Billy crumbled under the weight of the realization, falling to the ground and wailing at the relentless sun. He was sure he was going to die alone out there in the middle of the desert, and he let out all his terror and frustration, screaming and bawling, pounding the ground with his fists until his hands bled. He pulled himself up to his knees and shouted at the horizon. And then, to his complete and utter disbelief, the horizon responded.

It was a rumbling at first, faint and distant, more of a feeling than a sound—a slight vibration in the ground, the feeling of something approaching. Something big. Then he saw it, distant, still on the horizon, but coming nearer. He saw it, but he didn't believe it.

Less than an hour ago, he swore that he had seen a lake shimmering in the distance. He had run to it with maniacal glee, believing the impossible: that there was a lake in the middle of the desert, that he was saved. He laughed as he ran, and he ran and he ran, but got no closer to the water. When his breath was ragged he doubted for just a second, and then the lake vanished. It had been a mirage.

And so Billy kneeled there, wondering what sort of trick his eyes were playing. A train, of all things. Why not a cold clear stream rushing toward him? Or, better yet, Jenny Martin on a horse loaded with canteens of water. But a train? Why had his mind concocted a train?

"I've lost my mind," the young man said, sitting down and staring agape at the train still approaching, a long plume of steam billowing from its stack. He began to chuckle. "Completely loco." The chuckle became a laugh. He fell onto his side, his eyes still glued on the train, laughing harder. "How much for a ride, sir?" He hollered, "I could really use a ride!" He was in rolling hysterics now, convinced that the sun had baked what little sense he ever had. *It isn't real*, he was thinking, even as the shrill whistle split the silence of the desert and the locomotive light made him squint. He was able to make out the details as it drew closer: the gleaming black locomotive, the sharpened slant of the cow-catcher, the wheels chugging closer and closer.

By the time the whistle sounded again, Billy was no longer laughing. Not only did the train look as real as any locomotive he had seen, but it was headed right for him, chugging along over dirt and rock without the benefit of tracks. The train may have been a physical impossibility, but now less than 100 yards away, it seemed real enough to do serious damage to Billy if he didn't get out of the way.

Standing in shock, he stepped aside as the locomotive came to a hissing halt right next to him. The engineer leaned out the cabin with a sweaty grin under a grimy brown mustache. "Hey there, boy. Hope you don't mind me sayin' but you're looking right lost." Billy opened his mouth to speak, but all he could get out was a dry croak. "Seems to me you could use some help," the engineer continued. "We're going across the Playa, you interested in a lift?"

Billy rubbed his eyes and tried to speak again, but still wasn't able to get anything out. "Well, say something, boy! We don't got all day—running behind as it is!" When it became clear that Billy wasn't going to be able to speak any time soon, the exasperated engineer called out to someone in the car behind the locomotive. "Help me out with this one, won't you?" he shouted. "We don't have time for this kinda hold up!"

A conductor stepped out of the lead passenger car, smoothing back his slick black hair and putting on his conductor's hat. He didn't look at Billy directly, but puffed up his chest and shouted, "All aboard!" even though there was no one there to heed the call besides Billy, who was standing mere yards away, rooted there in stupefaction. The conductor saw that Billy wasn't going to move of his own accord and, with a sigh, walked over to him and practically carried him onto the train. The heavy slamming of the metal door and the sound of the steam engine's whistle as the train slowly heaved forward were the last things that he remembered.

"Reckon ya know what brought him out here?"

Billy heard the gruff voice, sounding close but also as though it was coming from a great distance. He opened his eyes, but all he could see were blurred shapes, browns, blacks and a point of dim, orange light. He was lying down on something soft—a bed.

"Who knows? Probably another one of those fool gold miners," another, younger-sounding voice said. "Found him out on the edge of town, half-dead. Miracle that he's even alive."

Everything came into focus all at once. Billy was lying in the corner of a room. The dim, orange blur was the flame of a kerosene lantern, the only source of light in the small chamber. There were two men standing by the door. One had a full gray beard, a stethoscope around his neck and a doctor's bag in his hand. The other was a younger man, wearing a holstered pistol hanging from a gun belt and a silver badge pinned to his vest. But all these were mere details next to the one looming fact. "I'm alive," Billy croaked, sitting up with a wince. His face was sunburned and blistered, and he felt as though his skin was tearing open when he spoke.

"Barely," the doctor said, walking to the bed. He took a glass of water from the bedside table and handed it to Billy. "Drink this slow, you hear? Your insides are dry as a prune."

The lawman stepped next to the doctor, looking vaguely amused as Billy coughed and spluttered at the first sip of water. "Damn fool, what were you doing out there, anyway?"

"Gold," Billy managed. "Looking for gold."

"Figures," the lawman said. "Let me guess—from Tombstone?"

"All right, all right," the doctor said, casting an irritated glance over his shoulder. "Boy just woke up. Give 'im a few minutes at least."

"Yeah," Billy rasped between gulps of water, "from Tombstone. Left for Dos Cabezas on Monday, last day of the month. Lost my burro and all my water my first night out. " The two men exchanged a look.

The doctor turned to Billy. "That's impossible, you're in Dos Cabezas now, and it's the morning of the second. No way anyone could make it across the Playa in two days."

"Must of cooked half his brains out on that desert," the lawman laughed. "Left on the last day of the month." He shook his head. "Poor jackass."

Billy put the glass down. "But I'm tellin' ya, that is when I left," he said. "I thought I was gone for sure." He stopped then, and looked at both the men carefully before continuing. "I was picked up, saved, by a train."

The lawman let out a snort. "Sorry, boy, not possible. Ain't no train that runs through the Playa. No such thing."

The doctor put a comforting hand on Billy's shoulder. "Not to worry, son. People are known to see all sorts of things when they're lost in the desert. It's normal."

Billy knew full well how crazy it sounded. He knew there was no such thing as trains that ran without tracks under their wheels. He knew that mirages were common out on the Playa, that a good many who crossed it swore they saw massive lakes where there was only rock and sand. Nevertheless, he stuck to his story. How else could he have reached Dos Cabezas in two days? Indeed, how else could he explain the fact that he was still alive?

But his continued insistence did nothing to sway the doctor or the peace officer. Neither was ready to put much stock in the words of a man who had endeavored to cross the Wilcox Playa on a rumor of gold—especially if that man was likely delusional from sunstroke. And yet despite the skepticism of the doctor and the peace officer, Billy's story would not die that day.

In fact, it became one of the better-known legends to emerge from the region. Although no one can say what, if anything, ended up happening between Billy Barclay and Jenny Martin, the tale of Billy's experience out on the Wilcox

Playa stuck. It started in Dos Cabezas and, within a matter of months, the story had spread through the whole region, told in every saloon, gambling house and brothel in Tombstone and Tucson, among cowboys while watching their herds and prospectors digging for their silver and gold.

Although the rumor that there was gold in the Wilcox Playa died soon after Billy's mysterious voyage from Tombstone to Dos Cabezas, there were a handful of individuals who made that difficult journey in the subsequent years. What accounts came from those wanderers? Were there any other sightings of a steam locomotive speeding through the desert? Did Billy Barclay's phantom train save any more lives?

Neither skeptics nor believers will be fully satisfied by the conclusion. For while no one actually *saw* a train rolling over the ground, more than one individual claimed to have *heard* one—a faint rumbling, the far-off sound of a whistle. Through the years, there have even been rumored sightings of a single light in the distance. It has only ever been reported at night, moving quickly across the horizon before vanishing into the darkness.

Are these sightings the result of overactive minds influenced by Billy Barclay's account, or could there actually be a phantom train that makes a regular trip through the Wilcox Playa? That depends on the credulity of the reader, and how much weight one allows supernatural folklore. Either way, the tale of the mysterious train continues to survive, though Billy Barclay seems to be the only person who has enjoyed the privilege of a ride.

The Ghosts in the Town Too Tough To Die

No one will mistake Tombstone, Arizona, for any kind of grand cultural center; nevertheless, this Cochise County town is still singular in the way its history so simply and brutally captures the American drive to make a buck. Situated on a scorched stretch of earth in the San Pedro Hills less than 20 miles from the Mexican border, Tombstone was founded in 1877 by Ed Schiefflin—a reckless prospector who stumbled upon a silver vein while on a practically suicidal hunt for mineral wealth. He named his claim "The Tombstone" to spite his detractors, who joked that the only thing he would find out in the Arizona desert was his own grave. The silver strike made Schiefflin into a millionaire, and thousands of prospectors hoping to emulate his success rushed into the region. So it was that the town of Tombstone practically sprang up overnight, crowding the recently bare region with young, hungry men, most with a love for whiskey and cards, all desperate to make a fortune.

It was the familiar story of the western boomtown—drunk and desperate fortune hunters with a shortage of prospects but overabundance of ambition. There were cowboys making their living off livestock in the surrounding countryside; there were miners burrowing deep into their dark pits for silver; and there were the denizens of the town of Tombstone itself, who provided all the usual frontier amenities to the men who swarmed into the region. Yet no other town was quite like Tombstone. The town's heyday cast an indelible mark on the cultural landscape of the American

Spirits from Tombstone's past still wander its deserted streets.

West. Of all the western boomtowns that took shape in the 19th century, it was Tombstone that would come to be celebrated as the embodiment of the freewheeling opportunism and violent confrontation that so often defined the Old West.

Cowboys, miners, gamblers, prostitutes, barkeepers, outlaws and lawmen—by 1898, there were over 10,000 people teeming through Tombstone's streets. Thousands of individuals came from all corners of the globe in search of the same thing: money. Some of these fortune hunters were more famous than others. As countless written pages and mile upon mile of film will attest, men like Virgil, Morgan and Wyatt Earp, Doc Holliday and Ike Clanton were frontier celebrities who are in no danger of being forgotten. The bloody vendetta between the Earps and the Clantons put the chaotic mining town into legend.

But Tombstone didn't become what it was solely through the misadventures of a small group of six-gun luminaries. The town's infamous lawlessness was created one bottle of whiskey at a time. It grew with every frustrated miner who finished a long day of grueling and fruitless labor; with every hard-earned dollar lost in one of the saloons; with every insult, real or imagined, directed at another armed young man far too jealous of his honor. Simply put, Tombstone suffered from too many men with too many guns drinking too much booze. Is it any wonder, then, that this town is said to be full of ghosts?

The Spirits in the Bird Cage Theatre

There is no disputing the Bird Cage Theatre's place as the most famous building in Tombstone. The notorious theater was established in 1881 and remained open until 1889, when flooded mines and sinking silver prices sent miners packing as quickly as they had arrived, reducing Tombstone to a virtual ghost town. But during the nine years that it was open, the Bird Cage Theatre was acknowledged as the fiery epicenter of Tombstone's chaos, packed night after night with the worst men in the region and earning a reputation that went beyond the parched deserts of the Southwest. In 1882 the

New York Times described the Bird Cage as the "wildest wickedest night spot between Basin Street and the Barbary Coast."

Every night, countless whiskey-soaked dramas would unfold under the orange, gas-lit glow within the lively theater. Maybe a lovesick miner would try his best to convince one of the house's prostitutes that she should leave her life of sin and join him on his claim as his wife, no matter what the owner of the house said. Perhaps an inebriated gunslinger would glare at a long-hated rival, his left hand steady on a fan of cards, his right moving slowly to the revolver at his hip. One stunned miner would win a fortune in a single game of faro, while another luckless gambler would watch in despair as he lost a year of his earnings with one misplaced bet. And in the 14 curtained cribs hanging over it all, ladies of the night would ply their immoral trade. It was a place where raw emotion mixed with limitless possibility, crushing disappointment and barrel upon barrel of rotgut whiskey. The outcome was often violent. There are over 140 bullet holes in the walls and ceiling of the Bird Cage, the result of the 16 gunfights said to have taken place there.

It might not come as such a surprise, then, that the Bird Cage Theatre is considered one of the most haunted places in town. Today, the Bird Cage is a museum, offering an immaculately preserved exhibition of Tombstone's wilder years. Many would say that it offers much more. The first accounts of strange happenings in the theater began shortly after it was reopened to the public in 1934. Closed since the last patron threw back his last glass of whiskey in 1889, the theater had been abandoned for nearly half a century. It quickly

The Bird Cage Theatre was the "wildest wickedest night spot between Basin Street and the Barbary Coast."

became apparent, however, that there were forces in the Bird Cage unconcerned with the passage of time.

The first visitors to the former theater-turned-museum were treated to an impressive array of artifacts from a time long past, but many of these early western enthusiasts were far more impressed by the bizarre and frightening phenomena occurring in the building. We can imagine their surprise when the sound of some distant carousing filled the otherwise quiet building. Faint but rowdy, boisterous laughter was heard, along with drunken voices singing old folksongs. There was also a distinct smell of cigar smoke on the air.

Many among this first wave of visitors would make their way downstairs, sure that some kind of celebration was going on in the basement. Yet all that greeted them when they got there was the empty Poker Room, where the longest poker game of all time—lasting a bewildering eight years, five months and three days—was said to have gone on during the 1880s. Though the sounds of distant revelry ceased the moment visitors opened the door, rattled witnesses would later swear that there was something intangibly eerie about the silence in the room—the way the light hung over the unoccupied table and chairs was frightening. There was a feeling that somehow, those chairs *were* occupied, with gamblers waiting for these intruders to leave before continuing with their game.

Other visitors claimed to hear the sound of a woman singing faintly in one of the second-floor cribs that overlooked the main room. The singing would grow louder, clearer, as witnesses climbed to the second floor, only to stop abruptly the moment anyone got too close to the cribs. There were other reports as well. People spoke of spur-jangling footsteps moving across the main room on the first floor when there was no one else there. On occasion, the disembodied footsteps would come incredibly close to visitors, passing within mere inches, yet still invisible to human eyes. Or, rather, to *most* human eyes. For there were also those who claimed to spot the purported phantom as he made his way across the Bird Cage's main room. He appeared as a semi-transparent figure in a black suit, with a big black cowboy hat perched on his head. Those able to see him have generally said that his hair is as black as his hat, and that he walks across the room with an easy stride, always vanishing before anyone is able to discern too much more.

Things at the Bird Cage haven't changed that much since the building was reopened in 1934. Now, as then, a number of individuals always claim to get much more out of their visit than they expected. Indeed, the bizarre sights and sounds have remained remarkably consistent over the last century. For the most part, what was reported then is still reported today, evidence that something still survives of the reckless carousing that once went on in the old Bird Cage Theatre.

Karen, Tracy and Charlie

Karen Carter grew up in the state of Virginia. She moved to Tombstone in 1992 after her family doctor told her the dry Arizona air would relieve her son's asthma. She spent the next three years there, making a modest living waiting on tables at the Bell Union Restaurant in the Bell Union Building on 4th and Fremont. She returned to Virginia in 1995 with a healthy Arizona tan and several bizarre stories.

Karen counts her experiences at the Bell Union among her most memorable during her stay in Tombstone.

"I hadn't been working in Bell Union for too long when I got wise to the strange things going on there," Karen says today. "It happened one night after closing. Tracy, a friend and coworker, was there with me. We were in the dining room, just about to start up our closing duties when it started."

Karen and Tracy were busy moving chairs when the silverware on every table began to shake. At first, the carefully arranged cutlery moved with a barely perceptible vibration, but within a matter of minutes, every fork, knife and spoon in the restaurant was jumping inches off the tables, rattling in a frightful cacophony. "Well, of course we were terrified," Karen says, "and without really thinking, both of us ran out of the dining room and into the kitchen."

Whatever reprieve the pair found there didn't last long. "We weren't in the kitchen for more than a minute or two before the dishwasher door slammed shut and started running all by itself. Me and Tracy were standing right there when it happened. Both of us could see that there was no one in front of the dishwasher." That was when Karen and Tracy decided that they had had enough. The owners lived in an apartment at the back of the building, and the pair ran down the hall to the apartment entrance, banging on the door in frightened desperation. Neither of the owners was home, but the short time away from the restaurant allowed the two women to collect their thoughts.

"Well, after a few minutes out in the hallway, me and Tracy got to laughing at ourselves. We talked about what had just happened, and sort of convinced ourselves that we might've overreacted a little bit." The pair walked carefully back into the restaurant, and saw that though the dishwasher was still running, the dining room was totally quiet. Relieved that things seemed to have gone back to normal, Karen and Tracy decided to get back to work. "Well, we ended up not getting much done," Karen says. "We were just getting started when I told Tracy that I was going to brew some coffee. The moment I said it, the coffee maker started all by itself. Water just started pouring out of the percolator. There was no pot underneath, and the water was overflowing onto the counter." Too frightened to stop the coffee machine, or even put a pot underneath it, the pair bolted out the front, locked the door behind them, and called it a night.

The next morning, Karen expected to be in some trouble when she came into work, seeing as how she and Tracy had left the place in a mess the night before. "Both owners, Jim and Dave, were there when I got to work the next day, cleaning the place up. I was surprised at how good they were taking it, but I was much more surprised at their reaction when I told them what happened the night before."

"So," Jim said to Karen, laughing, "you've met Charlie."

"Charlie," Karen soon found out, was the ghost that had been haunting the Bell Union Building for as long as anyone could remember. Quite a few different businesses had occupied the Bell Union since it was built in the early 1880s. In the first few years it was open, it housed the town's post office. Then it was purchased by a recently arrived Chinese entrepreneur who promptly turned the place into one of Tombstone's seediest establishments. Seedy in 1890s Tombstone would have translated into downright rotten anywhere else, yet the reputation of the Bell Union opium den was such that even some of the town's worst made it a habit to stay away. Thanks to the law, however, the drug house wasn't open for long.

The opium den's proprietor met his end soon after he opened the place. According to legend, he and a friend, both opium-addled, got the idea that a knife-throwing contest would be a lot of fun. One thing led to another, and in all the time it took for a knife to fly across the room, the Bell Union's owner found himself on the floor with a bowie knife jutting from his chest. He was dead before the opium in his blood stream wore off.

While the opium den owner faded in Tombstone's memory as quickly as weeds grew over his grave, everyone who worked at the Bell Union was reminded of him on a near-weekly basis. For they were convinced that this man's spirit was haunting their restaurant. His activities were sporadic and unpredictable. Sometimes, his ghost would be content enough to unravel the toilet paper, open and close doors or fool around with the lights. But on other occasions, his behavior would be far more dramatic.

Karen recalls her most frightening run-in with Charlie: "Well, it was the end of another shift, and me and Tracy were in late, cleaning the place up. The place was totally closed up; I mean, there was no one in there besides Tracy and me, and all the doors were locked. So we were cleaning up in the dining room again, when this man suddenly appears out of nowhere. He was a Chinese man, but he wasn't wearing the clothes that so many of the Chinese seemed to wear back then: he looked just like a cowboy, dressed up in a dirty old outfit, with a long coat and a banged up cowboy hat."

Karen and Tracy had become accustomed to Charlie's pranks, but this sighting was more than either of them had bargained for. This man looked as real as anyone walking down Allen Street on any given day. "He walked around the bar, looked at us once and then went on through the swinging doors that led to the back hallway." Karen and Tracy may have become used to the strange things that were going on in the restaurant; this incident, however, was too hard to overlook. Trying to convince herself that this man was an intruder, Karen called the police. Yet the ensuing investigation only confirmed that inexplicable things were afoot at the Bell Union.

"When the police got there, they found no evidence of a forced entry," Karen says. "All the doors were still locked and intact, and the Chinese cowboy that we saw was nowhere to be found. He wasn't in the back hallway, in either of the bathrooms or in the kitchen. And the door to Jim's apartment was still locked, so they decided he wasn't in there either." But the police were wrong in thinking that that this intruder would be impeded by any lock or door. "When Jim got home later on that night, his was place was completely trashed," Karen says. "His clothes were strewn all over the place; his furniture was upended; his papers were everywhere. The place was a complete mess."

Yet Jim knew better than to call the authorities. Years of experience with Charlie had forced him to accept the occasional fit of domestic carnage. Karen, as well, learned to put up with the Chinese ghost. Though Charlie would never again appear in front of her the way he did that night, he always made sure that not too much time elapsed without another prank. Most of them were minor incidents. In the three years that Karen worked in the Bell Union, a week never went by without the radio changing stations by itself, candles lighting on their own or water running by itself. Karen eventually got used to Charlie, and often addressed him like she would anyone else in the Bell Union. And unlike the reaction of so many other people to encounters with the supernatural, Karen laughs when she looks back at her experiences in Tombstone. "Charlie just wasn't ready to say 'bye' to the Bell Union. I guess that's why his spirit is still there today."

The Colfax County Dead

What used to be the town of Dawson lies in the Sangre de Cristo Mountains in Colfax County, New Mexico, some 15 miles northeast of the town of Cimarron. There isn't much left of the once-bustling coal mining community. Accessible by a single dirt road branching off Highway 64, Dawson is in the middle of a dusty nowhere, overrun by sagebrush and rattlesnakes. The only indications that the town ever stood are a commemorative placard situated on the abandoned town site and the Dawson Cemetery, a burial ground still marked by an old iron fence. The placard is a state historical marker telling an abridged version of the ghost town's short history, while the Dawson Cemetery is a plot of earth riddled with far too many identical white crosses, which, some would say, whisper a story all their own.

Unlike so many mining towns before it that sprang up around mineral wealth, Dawson was distinctly modern in that it was carefully planned and financed by a single corporation. The site was purchased in 1867 by a rancher named J.B. Dawson, who operated a ranch there until 1901, when the Dawson Fuel Company purchased the 20,000 acres with the intention of capitalizing on an enormous coal seam that had been discovered on a nearby mountain. But it wasn't until 1903, when Phelps Dodge bought the land, that the town of Dawson was born.

At its peak, Dawson boasted nearly 9000 residents. The Phelps Dodge Company oversaw the construction of homes for its workers and their families. There were schools for the children, fully staffed hospitals, an opera house for culture and a bowling alley for entertainment. At its peak, Dawson was a shining example of what a mining community could be. A far cry from the Leadvilles, Deadwoods and San Franciscos of the world, Dawson marked the end of the murderous madness that accompanied most mining towns of the American West. Nevertheless, when death came to Dawson, it came on a scale that put every other violent frontier town to shame.

Disaster struck on October 22, 1913. A faulty dynamite charge blew the insides out of one of the mines, killing almost everyone inside. By the time all the bodies were accounted for, it was determined that 263 men had perished in the explosion. It was one of the worst mining disasters in American history. The victims were buried in a special part of the Dawson Cemetery, their anonymous graves marked with small iron crosses.

From then on, Dawson's graveyard loomed larger in the public consciousness than the town itself. Whatever the people of Dawson were doing day to day, no one could ignore the sprawling stretch of corpses on the side of the mountain. No Boot Hill in any western town could compete with the air of death and desolation that hung over the town cemetery. The graveyard eventually seemed to take on a life of its own, and no one in Dawson was ever the same because of it. Soon after the disaster, frightening stories began to spread through the town. Some heard strange sounds—unlike anything produced by crickets or coyotes—drifting down from the graveyard, long lingering wails or moans that would come and go throughout the night. Others passing by the cemetery gates after sunset claimed to see dim, humanoid shapes walking through the darkness, vague forms that vanished the moment anyone tried to take a closer look.

Citizens of Dawson quickly decided that their cemetery was haunted. Locals assumed that the graveyard was full of miners' spirits that were angry or confused at their sudden and needless deaths. Looking back, however, it might be said that the ghosts of Dawson Cemetery were trying to warn the living. For on February 8, 1923, 10 years after the first mining accident broke Dawson's heart, another explosion tore through a crowded mine. And another 123 miners gave up their lives digging for coal.

The men's remains were dug out of the rubble and buried alongside the bodies from the 1913 disaster, identical small iron crosses marking the graves of the nameless dead. So it was that two of the worst mining disasters in the United States' history took place in a humble New Mexico town. The Dawson Cemetery, now bristling with 386 miners' crosses, became a monument to Dawson's darker side. After 1923, whatever went on within the town itself was overshadowed by the specter of death that hung over the graveyard.

It's fitting, then, that curiosity seekers looking for the mining town in northern New Mexico today will find only the desolate Dawson Cemetery. While the rest of the original buildings in the town are either torn down or now located on private property, the cemetery is open to anyone who cares to see it. The iron gate to the burial ground still stands under the blazing southwestern sun, its metal letters, spelling "DAWSON," somehow ominous on the lonely mountain. And unlike the residents of the mining town, who left the borough shortly after Phelps Dodge shut down the mines in 1950, the ghosts of the Dawson Cemetery have remained behind.

Dawson Cemetery

There are countless stories of strange happenings in the graveyard. Daytime visitors often claim to have heard barely audible whispers on the wind, the voices of men warning of some unseen and unfathomable danger. Others speak of fierce cold spots that surround specific gravesites: people who were sweating a few moments before find themselves shivering in the sudden chill. The cold spell lasts for a few short moments before lifting without warning, leaving witnesses frightened and confused, wondering what exactly they had just experienced.

But the most dramatic accounts of ghosts in the Dawson Cemetery are set during the evening hours. That is when the daytime whispers become full-throated moans drifting over the burial ground. Curiosity seekers and investigators have witnessed balls of light floating over the expanse of iron crosses. Some claim to have spotted vaguely human-shaped patches of glowing fog drifting through the graveyard. The forms hover for a few moments before dissipating into the night air, leaving no trace that they were ever there.

It might be more suitable to call the dead of Dawson Cemetery corporate casualties rather than men who were felled by the violence of the Old West. They were, after all, employees of Phelps Dodge—men who were taken care of by the company that settled them, men who never had to worry about gunfighters, cowboys or Indians. Yet the miners of Dawson risked their lives to make a buck, and in the end, for 386 of them, their rough jobs on the hard periphery of the United States cost them their lives. They still don't seem too happy about it.

Ghosts of the Yuma Territorial Prison

Death is the tyrant that strikes fear into the hearts of most of the convicts. It means those that are not claimed and are without friends will lie beneath the barren plot just outside the penitentiary—the convict's cemetery. Piles of rock shaped like a grave with a plain slab giving the name and number mark the final resting place. Services are brief at a convict's funeral. There are no mourners, no tears, no flowers— a simple burial service by a minister or priest, and that is all.

—*The Tucson Citizen*, November 24, 1906

The Yuma Territorial Prison had been open for over 30 years when this bleak account of death within the isolated penitentiary was penned by a Tucson journalist. By then, it was clear that the old rock and adobe prison was nearing the end of its service. Crumbling and overcrowded, the old prison was a physical reminder of a bygone age—a relic from a time when there were more tumbleweeds than people in the southwestern corner of the country, and justice was just as likely to be administered with the wrong end of a six-shooter as it was through due process of law.

The prison's first cells were built by seven unfortunate convicts from the Yuma County jail in the early summer of 1876. They were brought to the site throughout that May and

June, marched through the desert shackled and chained, supervised under gunpoint as they broke and piled rock to form their own prison cells in the middle of the Yuma Desert. We can only imagine what these men must have been thinking as they groaned and sweated under the sweltering heat, constructing the walls that would soon enclose them.

These cells were finished on July 1 that year, just in time for monsoon season. The seven convicts who built and occupied the prison's first cells were forced to put up with the extremities of the Yuma Desert's harsh climate, where temperatures could get as high as 120°F in midday, turning their small cluster of adobe cells into sun-baked ovens. When the rain came, water thundered down on the cells, pouring in through every crack in the poorly constructed building. A stay in the Yuma Prison was hardly luxurious. Over the years, the prison grew with the number of convicts in the territory: cells were constructed to accommodate the increasing number of badmen that were riding into the Yuma Territory.

Every sort of person did time in the cramped cells. There were murderers, robbers, swindlers and perverts; drunkards and gamblers; victims and innocents. While the prison was active, 3069 prisoners, 29 of them women, served sentences inside its walls. Not everyone made it out of the prison alive. One hundred and eleven convicts would die in their cells, looking out at the world through barred windows during the last moments of their lives. It is believed that some of the spirits of these unlucky few still haunt the Yuma Territorial Prison, which operates today as one of Arizona's state historic parks.

Many believe the ghost of John Ryan to be the most active spirit that haunts the former prison. No one can say who saw him first. It may have been a tourist wandering through the park in the not-too-distant past, or it may have been a convict unlucky enough to be thrown into cell 14 when the penitentiary was still being used. Whatever the case, Ryan's ghost manifested itself the way it always has: a faint white figure pacing within the darkness of the cell, two dimly shining eyes, the sound of nervous footsteps walking back and forth, a sudden drop in temperature.

John Ryan was the first man to die in the Yuma Territorial Prison. As depraved a man as the West had ever produced, Ryan wandered in from Iowa during the 1890s, trying to make his way as a miner on the frontier. He was successful enough at this endeavor to start a family, getting married shortly after arriving and fathering three children with his young wife. Well, you can take the man out of the place, but you can't take the devil out of the man, and whatever inner-demons John Ryan thought he left behind in Iowa came back with a vengeance on the wild periphery of the Southwest.

Ryan fell into debauchery soon after his third child was born, spending more and more time at the nearest saloon filling his gut with acrid frontier whiskey and gambling away what little money he had. We can only guess at what kind of madness possessed him, but by the end of 1899, he hit rock bottom. The record shows only that he was arrested for committing a "crime against nature" and was sentenced to five years in the Yuma Territorial Prison on September 28, 1900.

Where some murderers, robbers and con-artists might have received a certain degree of respect in western jail houses, men who were in for the sort of crimes that Ryan was accused of were made targets among the outlaw population. Mercilessly harassed and mortally threatened by the other

The unique rock and adobe prison housed bad frontier men—robbers, swindlers, drunkards, gamblers—who were unlucky enough to have been caught.

inmates in the Yuma jail, Ryan was quickly separated from the rest of the prisoners for his own safety. But in reality there was no safe place for John Ryan, because when all was said and done, he was his own worst enemy.

The three years Ryan occupied cell 14 could hardly have been called tranquil. Perpetually pacing through the darkness of his cell, Ryan was always awake, often spending his evening hours roaring every profanity a man can utter into the darkness. More than once, his rants resulted in his banishment into the "Dark Cell," where he suffered solitary confinement in complete darkness for days at a time. By March 31, 1903, Ryan's unknown demons finally got the better of him. He was found in his cell, hanging by the neck from a rope he made with the blankets in his room.

Yet this wasn't the last the world would hear of John Ryan. Throughout the years, the strange sights and sounds plaguing cell 14 have repeatedly brought the name of the tortured frontiersman to the lips of the living. It is widely believed that Ryan's ghost is largely responsible for the strange occurrences there. Though the Yuma Territorial Prison was shut down on September 15, 1909, roughly six years after Ryan passed away, it has never really been completely abandoned. Throughout the 1920s and 1930s, the prison was used as a shelter by hobos and the homeless; during the following years, locals took to cannibalizing parts of the compound for building materials.

In the more recent past, the former prison has become something of a tourist attraction. The old prison complex is now a registered state historic park. It is the experiences of these visitors in and around cell 14 that have turned John Ryan from another sad story of the Old West to one of the region's most popular ghosts.

People walking by cell 14 have heard the shuffling sounds coming from the darkness of the barred room. Many of those who stop to take a closer look see nothing in the cell, the sound of someone's manic pacing suddenly replaced by silence. While this has caused more than one visitor to doubt his senses, others stopping before cell 14 have been subjected to sights, sounds and sensations strange enough to impel them to doubt their own sanity. These are the people who have looked upon the ghost of John Ryan.

Run-ins with this apparition are usually described in the same fashion. Witnesses feel an abrupt drop of temperature as they peer into the cell, and then—sometimes gradually, sometimes suddenly—he appears out of thin air. He appears in the back of the cell, a shadowy silhouette pacing across the width of the room, his only recognizable feature being two white lights shining faintly where his eyes should be. There one moment, gone the next, the ghost of John Ryan is never visible for more than a few seconds before vanishing from sight completely, leaving cell 14 as empty as it was mere moments before.

Jesse Torres, an employee at the Yuma Territorial Prison State Historic Park, considers himself a skeptical man, not prone to buying into fantastical stories of the ghosts of tortured convicts. Nonetheless, he admits that there is something strange about cell 14. "There've been times when I've walked by the cells and gotten this eerie feeling. It's like, the temperature drops and something feels not quite right. I don't know if I believe in ghosts, but this has happened to me more than once." Rationalizing the experience, Jesse says that it may well be a figment of his imagination, but even as the words come out of his mouth, he sounds slightly uncertain. He concludes his account of cell 14 by falling back on historical fact, concrete information he can rely on. "Whatever the case, John Ryan was an all-around bad man, so bad that none of the other inmates wanted anything to do with him."

Has the inborn evil that tortured Ryan while he was alive remained in cell 14? Is this what some witnesses are seeing when they peer through the iron bars? Is this what Jesse Torres feels when he walks by the long-abandoned room? Or is Ryan's ghost a paranormal expression of his earthly agony, a sort of psychic imprint left behind in the same cell he spent the last years of his life in? Whatever the case, John Ryan, who lived most of his life in bitter anonymity, could never have guessed that people would be talking about him in the 21st century. But as long as the apparition continues to haunt cell 14 in the Yuma Territorial Prison, this poor outlaw's morbid tale will not be allowed to rest.

The Ghost of Tom Wright

Henry Lambert stared at the five cards in front of him, trying his best to stop a smile from creeping to the corners of his mouth. There were five hearts in his hands, arranged in order from six to ten—a straight flush. Lambert let his eyes wander to the five other men sitting around the table, going from one man to the next, until they stopped on the famous Thomas Wright, one of the most celebrated card players on the frontier. *Here I am, out in New Mexico,* Lambert thought to himself, *playing poker at a high stakes table with the one-and-only Tom Wright, and I've got a straight flush in my hands.*

As far as Lambert was concerned, things couldn't get any better. *God knows, it's been long enough coming,* he thought to himself as he looked around at the drunken revelry in his packed Cimarron saloon, *but I've finally made it.* The blithe Frenchman downed a shot of whiskey and looked back at the table, which was groaning under the weight of the cash, gold and personal valuables gathered in the center. He looked at his cards again and smiled. *All mine.*

A French emigrant who had had taken the trip across the Atlantic in the 1850s, Lambert was a young man when he arrived in the United States with his head full of romantic notions about the American West. He had left France determined to test his mettle in the wide-open wildness of the American frontier. Fanciful notions of the savage nobility of American Indians, the unrefined gallantry of Texans and the limitless possibilities of the western horizon were dancing through his mind. Henry made a promise to himself that as soon as he saved enough money to make the passage, he would try his luck in the California gold fields.

Fate, however, had different plans for him. Henry Lambert had one talent that elevated him above other men, and it wasn't toughness, skill at cards, or proficiency with a six-shooter. Henry Lambert could cook. The young Frenchman was only in his 20s, but he had yet to meet a man who could throw together a better meal than he. Lambert was an artist, a genius, and anyone who tried his foie gras, glazed duck or quails eggs in Hollandaise sauce would be hard pressed to disagree.

Of course, Lambert didn't think that such a skill would serve him well on the rough fringes of frontier America; he intended to use his talent purely as a means to get him to California. With exactly this purpose in mind, Henry got work in an upscale New York restaurant, but it wouldn't be that simple. The moment wealthy New Yorkers got a taste of Lambert's prodigious talents, he was elevated to culinary stardom. Every night, people clamored to get into the establishment where Henry cooked. Quickly gaining a reputation as one of the most gifted chefs in the city, Lambert attracted the attention of the wealthiest and most powerful in New York society.

Three years flew by in money-soaked succession, and before he was able to really take stock of his meteoric success, the young French chef was offered the job of personal cook for none other than the president of the United States. And so it was that Henry Lambert began managing the White House kitchen when Abraham Lincoln won the presidency in 1860. Lambert cooked for the president for the next five years, pulling together the best meals he could for Lincoln while the Civil War raged across the United States. Who knows how long he would have remained in Washington,

D.C., had things not turned out they way they did. His dreams of lighting out West had become a distant fantasy entertained by a much younger version of himself during his years at the White House, but they come back strong in 1865. The very day it was announced that President Lincoln was dead, Lambert quit his job and left, turning his back on the East forever.

Yet the hopes he had for a striking it rich in the hills of northern California were thwarted. While Henry was a brilliant chef, as a gold prospector he was inexperienced, uninformed and just plain unlucky. Having been conned, robbed and hoodwinked by every confidence man, highwayman and six-gun ne'er-do-well he had come across, Lambert was destitute within a year of arriving in Sacramento. It turned out that the West wasn't nearly so grand has he had dreamed. So, without a dollar or gold nugget to his name, Lambert went back to doing what he did best.

The once-famous chef got work in a San Francisco eatery, and promptly began making magic of the local fare. Apparently, his skills weren't lost on the rough palates of frontier men, and the establishment he worked at was soon bursting at the rafters with every gambler, gunfighter and gold digger that could fit in the building. One of the customers, a wealthy New Mexican financier, enjoyed his meal so much that he walked into the kitchen after he was finished and offered Lambert an exorbitant sum to be his personal cook. Lambert didn't have to think about it very long; taking a final look at the cramped and chaotic kitchen he worked in, the chef walked out with his new employer and took the next train out to Cimarron, New Mexico.

The White House kitchen

He made more money working for his new employer than he did working for the president, and after a few years Henry had saved up a substantial sum. It was then that the master chef decided to open up an establishment of his own. Lambert's Saloon and Billiard Club opened in the late 1870s, and Henry suddenly found himself in the position to cook his goose's golden eggs and indulge his lifelong fascination with the Wild West. For Henry's saloon did a raucous business in the bustling town of Cimarron, which was located on the last stretch of the Santa Fe Trail.

Lambert's establishment bore hardly any resemblance to past eateries he had worked in. More a frontier drinking room than a restaurant, Lambert's selection of whiskies and ales dwarfed his sparse menu of French cuisine. Most of the men that stepped into his saloon were more interested in cards and booze than fine food, and it wasn't long before Lambert's Saloon became a famous gathering place for some of the worst men the Southwest had to offer. After only a few years of business, Lambert's operation was so successful that he added 30 hotel rooms and renamed it the St. James Hotel. The most infamous of the Old West's perfidious pantheon would eventually walk through the St. James' front door— men such as Jesse James, Clay Allison, Wyatt Earp, Billy the Kid and Pat Garret all spent time under Lambert's roof at one time or another.

In time, Lambert traded in his spatula for a six-shooter and took to joining his dubious celebrity guests for booze and cards, fancying himself an honorary member of the six-gun brotherhood that whooped it up in his bar nightly. He was probably the most permissive barkeeper in all of Cimarron, and it is said that 26 men were killed in drunken shootouts that erupted within the saloon. Legend has it that the ceiling had to be replaced after the first couple of years because of the 400-some bullet holes punched through it.

Lambert was probably happiest during this period of his life. Laughing, drinking and gambling with the same scoundrels he worshipped, the former cook drank up the company of these frontiersmen with unbridled zeal. But like all good things, his days under the western sun did not last. The end of his glory days came quickly, in all the time it takes for a man to throw down five cards on a table.

Though Thomas Wright carried a six-shooter, he never used it. One of the more accomplished gamblers west of the Mississippi, Wright made his living at the card tables across the frontier. He played in practically every gambling house from Tombstone to Dodge City, and was known for his fair play and his outsized personality. So it was that Wright was one of the few men who could boast at having won the last dollar off murderous gamblers like Ben Thompson and Doc Holliday without a single altercation. He couldn't have imagined his clean track record was about to change when he was introduced to a drunk and merry Henry Lambert, who gave Wright an affectionate hug when he met him.

For that matter, Lambert couldn't have imagined it either. Indeed, with the six-to-ten straight flush in his hand, he couldn't imagine anything besides the small fortune he was about to win—about to win, no less, from Thomas Wright. The pot built steadily as the bets went around the table. Men threw in 100-dollar bills, watches, gold nuggets, jewels—by the time it came around to Lambert for the second time, the chef decided to make a grand statement about the cards in his hand. Basking in the attention of the spectators, the soused man let a moment of dramatic silence pass before he made his bet. "I would like to bet the title deed of this hotel."

Much to Lambert's delight, a collective gasp went through the gambling room, as if the St. James itself had drawn its breath in disbelief. By the time the chef wrote up a hasty deed on a piece of paper, all of the other men at the table had folded, unable or unwilling to match the excessive bet. All, that is, except Tom Wright.

Eyeing up Henry Lambert with a lopsided grin stretched across his face, Wright reached into his jacket pocket and pulled out a wad of folded hundred-dollar bills that looked thick enough to stop a bullet. The legendary gambler paused for a moment before he threw the money down. "I wouldn't normally ask, but you sure you want to do this, Frenchy?"

Lambert felt beads of sweat forming on his brow in spite of himself. "You're bluffing," was all he could get out.

"So be it," Tom Wright said as he threw the cash onto the middle of the table. "I call."

Lambert laid his straight flush down, finally allowing his smile to break out into a joyful guffaw. "Beat that, y'old card shark!" he hollered at his opponent. Henry was just about to lean forward and grab his loot when Tom Wright threw his cards down. He had a royal flush: all spades.

"Nothing personal, Frenchy," Tom said to the suddenly pale chef, "but I'll be wanting you out of here by tomorrow. A bet's a bet, after all."

Wright reached forward to grab the loot, and Henry snapped. "You cheat!" the enraged Frenchman roared at his opponent. "There's no way you could've drawn a royal flush." Lambert was stammering as he spoke, unable to come to terms with his loss. When Wright made another movement

"You cheat!" the enraged Frenchman roared at his opponent.

to take his winnings, Lambert ordered two of his house thugs to hold him back. "Search his sleeves!" he yelled. "I'll bet anything he's got cards in his jacket."

"I wouldn't be making any more bets for a while if I were you," Wright said to Lambert as the two burly men rifled through his jacket. There were no cards on him. "Well, that settles it then," he said. "Fair and square, eh Pierre? I'm goin' upstairs to get some sleep."

"Get out of my hotel!" Lambert screamed at the professional gambler as he walked away.

"Hell, Henry, you can't kick me out of my own place," Tom answered over his shoulder.

A few men in the saloon laughed; Lambert flipped his lid. An instant later, the chef reached down to his hip with shaking hands, grabbed his gun and fired, blowing a hole through Tom Wright's back. Silence descended over the hotel as the patrons took in the spectacle of Wright in his death throes on the saloon floor. But no one was more shaken than the perpetrator of the capital crime. Unable to take in what he had just done, Lambert dropped his gun and dashed out of the saloon, leaving a writhing Tom Wright behind him. "Well," someone said, "we best take him to his room."

A few men stepped forward, lifted the dying man off the floor and took him to his hotel suite: room 18. Although Wright was a congenial man throughout his life, there was nothing graceful about the way he left the world. Thrashing violently in blood-soaked sheets, the gambler unleashed his pain and anger in a series of profane epithets, calling down the town of Cimarron, the establishment he was gunned down in and, most of all, the yellow-bellied Frenchman who shot him in the back. A doctor was called in to see if anything could be done, but Wright was quickly deemed beyond help. A priest followed, intent on giving the dying man his last rites, but Tom pulled his revolver and shouted every curse he could think of at the rapidly retreating parson. "Hellfire if my soul ain't damned beyond any prayer!" the livid man shrieked at the holy man's back. "But by Lucifer and his burning host, I swear I'll come back to torment that lousy Frenchman! I swear it!" At that moment, there wasn't a man in the hotel who didn't believe him. Tom was dead before the night was up.

Lambert returned to his hotel after a brief hiatus, planning on managing the establishment again. But things at the St. James would never be the same. For one, Henry Lambert had lost his jovial air. No longer did patrons hear his delirious laughter ring through the hotel on crowded nights; no longer did he walk amongst his frontier clientele with his put-on swagger, pressing palms and buying drinks. Indeed, Lambert spent more and more time in the confines of his kitchen, sitting in silence for entire evenings with a bottle of whiskey in his hands. In the end, this eager western enthusiast found his own frontier experience too much to digest, and the rest of his days were spent in a haunted, heavy silence.

But Lambert wasn't the only one who was haunted by the deceased gambler. Soon after Tom Wright died, employees and patrons of the St. James Hotel became convinced that the dead man's spirit remained in the hotel to see through his dying curse. His presence was said to be especially strong in the first few years after his death. Employees would tell stories about being struck by some invisible force while they were working, and bottles of booze frequently flew off shelves and across the room, shattering against the barroom walls. It wasn't uncommon for men playing cards at the table where Wright was dealt his last hand to bolt out of their seats and run out of the hotel screaming, later saying that they had felt a pair of ice-cold hands close around their throats.

Yet of all the strange things that occurred, the most terrifying phenomena occurred in room 18. Patrons unfortunate enough to sleep in room 18 would never make it through the night. Invariably, they would come running out sometime in the early hours with a story about "the angry man at the foot of the bed" or the thick cloud of menacing mist that floated through the room, turning the bedchamber into a veritable ice box. It wasn't long before Lambert had the room locked up for good; but even then, those suites adjacent to the cursed room had their fair share of strange occurrences, and Lambert would warn guests staying in them about the unfriendly ghost that was known to appear there.

Things went from bad to worse at the St. James Hotel. As the phenomena in the hotel intensified, Tom Wright's last words took on the weight of legend. "It's the spirit of Tom Wright up there in room 18," locals would say. "He said he'd come back from the dead to stick it to ol' Lambert; I guess that's what he's done." Others offered theories on the dead gambler's determination to see that Lambert made good on his bet, saying that if Wright couldn't take what was owed him in life, his spirit would do his darndest after death. And maybe Wright would have driven Lambert out of the hotel if Lambert's wife, Mary, hadn't passed away when she did.

By all accounts, the paranormal activity at the St. James lessened considerably after Mary Lambert died. While strange and unpleasant things still occurred regularly in room 18, bottles stopped flying across the barroom, and the attacks on patrons dropped off dramatically. Wright's angry ghost stopped appearing in the rooms next to number 18. Moreover, other, more pleasant stories began circulating about the St. James. Employees grew conscious of a mysterious helper that would help them with the work around the hotel. Chambermaids walking into rooms they were about to clean would find beds made with crisp, clean sheets, while the dirty linens would be piled neatly beside the door. Dishes suddenly acquired a mysterious tendency to clean themselves. And Henry Lambert put away the bottle and took up cooking again, once more putting his talents to good use with the wide array of new dishes he put on the menu.

Guests noticed the change as well. Some said they spotted a kind-looking, middle-aged woman framed by a warm and comforting light. Anyone who spotted her would talk about the undeniable sense of well-being they felt when they saw her. Business picked up in the St. James Hotel once again and, while room 18 was still off-limits, the air around the locked door still whispering an intangible and ominous promise, there was almost no trace of the vicious spirit that haunted the hotel throughout much of the 1880s.

The popular theory is that the spirit of Mary Lambert, always kind and gentle while alive, had taken up residence in her husband's hotel after she died, hoping to help the poor man deal with the sins of his past. Somehow, she was able to ease Wright's angry presence with her own good-hearted influence. In this sense, the St. James became something of a paranormal battleground, where one woman's gentle ghost somehow manages to keep another, fiercely malevolent, spirit in check.

To this day, owners, employees and guests of the St. James have expressed awareness of this two-sided ghostly element in the hotel. On one hand, there is the darkness that resides in the still-barred room 18; on the other, there is the calming spirit of Mary Lambert who seems to have free reign over the rest of the building. Management has done everything it can to placate the angry Wright and keep Mary happy as well. Room 18 has been stocked with three of Tom Wright's

The calming spirit of Mary Lambert can still be felt within the St. James Hotel.

favorite things in the world: a pack of playing cards, a shot glass, and a bottle of Jack Daniel's. Meanwhile, guests staying in Mary Lambert's room are only told to make sure that they shut the window before they go to sleep. An open window is said to be the only thing that irritates Mary, who has been known to tap on the window until sleeping guests wake up and close it.

A small price to pay for protection from Tom Wright's vengeance.

Betrayal in the Anza Borrego

It was a clear night in the Anza Borrego Desert. Partially concealed behind an elevated outcropping of rock, four masked horsemen sat still and quiet, looking out on the starlit desert before them. A thin sliver of a moon was rising ominously over the sagebrush, dirt and rock of the California desert. Armed to the teeth with rifles, shotguns and revolvers, the riders waited, their eyes fixed on the distant road stretching across the desert below them.

One of the men shifted in his saddle, reached over his shoulder and scratched the back of his neck. He cast an irritated look at Luke, the one they called their leader. He was about to say something about how they had been waiting there for hours now for a stagecoach that was supposed to come rolling down that road. He was about to ask Luke if he was sure that this wagon was going to show, and if maybe it would be a better idea if they turned around and headed to Vallecito Station for whiskey and some cards. He opened his mouth, but the leader of the band cut him off before he could say a word, holding up a gloved hand for silence. Squinting hard into the darkness, Luke stood in his stirrups and leaned forward, trying to get a better look at whatever had caught his attention. "It's coming," he hissed through his bandana. "Get your guns."

There it was in the faint silver light—a dark speck on the road, moving across the grand vista, getting closer. The men drew their weapons, and there was a metallic *click* and *clack* of impending violence. Chambers loaded. Hammers cocked. A few more minutes, and the stagecoach was clearly visible; four horses, one teamster and one man riding shotgun. The bandits waited until the wagon was just below them before they put their spurs to their horses and descended on the coach. The infamous holdup in the Anza Borrego had begun.

It was the summer of 1857, and the bandits were riding down on a stagecoach said to be hauling $65,000 east to St. Louis. The plan was to take the loot and ride hard for Vallecito Station, a small rest stop several miles to the east. Once there, they were to divide the take four ways and split up for good, each lighting off with over $15,000 in his saddlebags. That was the plan anyway, but the heist in the Anza Borrego turned out to be a much more complicated affair— an ugly debacle of betrayal and bloodshed that left a stain on the desert that many believe remains today, manifested in the ghostly apparitions that appear in Vallecito Station.

"You shoot, you die!" Luke roared at the stagecoach guard, who was holding his shotgun in shaking hands, taking stock of the riders that had surrounded the wagon. Four guns against his one. He wouldn't stand a chance. His eyes went from the barrels of the guns trained on him, to the man driving the wagon, and decided that he wasn't ready to die for someone else's money. Slowly, he lowered his shotgun to the floorboards and raised his arms into the sky.

"That a boy," growled the leader. "Keep goin' with them instincts and you might make it through this." Keeping his gun trained steadily on the guard, the leader nodded at two of his confederates. The pair rode up to the wagon, shot the lock off the door and began emptying it, one bag at a time. They didn't stop until $65,000 in gold coins hung from their horses' saddles. Luke tipped his hat at the driver and the guard, and gave the word to his band. The four riders galloped away, their forms fading quickly in the darkness.

But they weren't going to make their getaway that easily. Infuriated, humiliated or emboldened when the riders galloped off, the stagecoach guard acted. He picked his shotgun up off the coach floor, took aim at the dim form of one of the riders and pulled the trigger. Enough of the shotgun blast found its mark, and the rider slumped lifeless in his saddle. He had been riding one of the horses that was loaded with gold, and Luke wheeled around to take the reins, leading it to where the two other bandits were waiting behind the outcropping of rock. It was quiet except for labored breath. One of the men had his bandana pulled down under his bearded chin.

"Sonuvabitch," the bearded man spat, cocking the lever of his rifle. "I say we ride back and kill them both." But neither of the two remaining men responded. A pregnant silence loomed behind the outcropping. "Well, what the hell are we waiting for!" the bearded man said, looking now somewhat frantically at his two companions. "Let's go!"

"Sorry, man," the leader said. " 'Fraid this is where it ends for you."

The bearded man hadn't seen the third man, Bill, train his pistol at the back of his head. But he did hear the hammer click. He did see the farewell in Luke's eyes. "Why you rotten…" He never got the chance to finish. Bill pulled the trigger, and then there were two.

"That about does it," said Luke. "Good shootin', Bill. I knew you had it in you."

"Sure," said Bill.

The two men got off their horses and mounted the ones carrying the gold. Leaving behind their dead cohorts, they rode away heading east toward Vallecito Station, stopping

The ugly debacle of betrayal and bloodshed left a stain on the desert.

somewhere along the way to bury the gold. And so the traitorous pair arrived at the small adobe structure ready to celebrate. The heist had ended as they'd planned, with their two confederates dead and $65,000 to split between the two of them. They were home free.

They took a small table in a shadowy corner and proceeded to throw back shot after shot of rotgut whiskey.

"Forget about 'em!" Bill was heard shouting at one point. "They were damn useless to us anyway."

"Well, thanks to those two, I'll never have to draw my gun again," Luke responded. "Ain't nothing but the good life for me now."

Luke could have no idea how mistaken he was. While murdering for money was nothing new to the pair, neither had committed such a betrayal before, and though they didn't know it, there was a price to be paid for such treachery. It wasn't long before their whiskey-fueled exuberance turned into besotted paranoia. Luke's casual glances around the room got Bill to wondering if a plot had been devised to get rid of him as well. He began to wonder if one of the patrons in the small station was also in on the plan, and was waiting for the quick nod, the look, the code word to finish the job. Soon he was unable to go five seconds without throwing worried glances over his shoulder. Drunk as Luke was, he began to notice his accomplice's sudden twitchiness, the constant glances across the room and the laughter that had grown forced, uneasy. The usually composed bandit leader became wary.

"What's gotten into you, man?" the drunken ringleader slurred. "You worried a priest is gonna show up?"

Bill looked closely at Luke, his eyes squinting. "Why is that?" he said. "I'm just taking a look around, you got somethin' 'gainst that?" He glared across the table through whisky eyelids. "Or are you hoping to catch me unawares?"

It was then that Luke saw the streak of hatred smeared across Bill's face, and was instantly reminded that his partner was packing a loaded Peacemaker at his hip. *The bastard intends to shoot me,* Luke thought as his hand fell under the table to where his own shooting iron was strapped. He asked his next question in slow, measured tones, his palm clasped tightly around the handle of his Colt 45. "You ain't thinking of doing anything stupid, are ya, Bill?"

Not another word was said. Bill jumped to his feet and hauled his revolver from its holster. But Luke was quicker. Still sitting, he skinned his gun first, firing two bullets into his partner's stomach before the man could get a single shot off. "Sorry, partner," the bandit leader said, getting up and walking toward the exit as Bill fell to the ground. The fight, however, was not quite over. Just as Bill began losing focus, his palm closed around the cool wood of his pistol handle. He raised the weapon and pulled the trigger. His bullet found its mark, and Luke fell dead at the threshold of the building. A moment later, Bill breathed his last as well as his blood spread across the Vallecito Station floor.

The stagecoach that the bandits had robbed arrived at Vallecito Station later that night, and it wasn't long before bystanders put the details of the gunfight together. That same night, almost everyone at the station went out looking for the buried gold, hoping to strike it rich on the bandits' ill-gotten gains. Yet no one found it. The story of the lost gold in the Anza Borrego spread throughout the West over the following years, and people came from all over looking for the buried treasure. Seasons became years, which turned to decades, and still, the gold of the Anza Borrego went unclaimed. Time turned the robbery and brutal murders into one of the legends of the Old West, and future generations saw the hidden gold in the desert as more of a folktale than a tangible treasure waiting to be discovered. But the promise of gold wasn't the only thing that made the heist near Vallecito into legend.

People began to talk about strange goings-on in Vallecito Station soon after the bandits murdered one another. The first of these reports came from passengers on the Butterfield Overland Stage. Established in 1858, the Butterfield Stage offered a route to travelers making the long trip between St. Louis and San Francisco. It was along this route that the Vallecito Station sat, built in an oasis in the Anza Borrego. While the Butterfield Overland Stage was in business, from 1858 to 1861, Vallecito Station saw its busiest time. And it was during this time that the legend of the phantom gunfighters was born.

To visitors stopping at the station during daylight hours, the spirits manifested themselves with disembodied footsteps—the sound of spurs jingling as an invisible presence makes its way to the adobe structure only to fall silent just before the doorway. Those sitting in the sweltering heat claimed to be seized by a sudden cold spell so severe that it made the hairs stand up on the back of necks and breath turn to visible vapor. The cold lasted only for several seconds, and occurred only in the same corner where Luke and Bill sat after they held up the stagecoach.

Visitors to the station during evening hours were in for even more startling experiences. The spirits of Vallecito seemed to acquire greater strength after the sun went down. It was then that Luke and Bill acquired visible form, appearing as faint apparitions to shocked travelers. Eyewitnesses could only stare at the slightly transparent image of Luke as he took two or three deliberate steps toward the door before vanishing at the threshold. Others looked horrified at the faintly luminescent form of Bill lying face down on the same ground where he fell.

The Civil War brought an end to business on the Butterfield Line. Vallecito Station was deserted, left to bake and forgotten in the southern California sun. In 1934 San Diego County purchased the station and surrounding oasis and rebuilt the crumbling building from its ruins. Vallecito was turned into a campground for motorists in the Anza Borrego—once more a rest stop for travelers. Apparently, the years did nothing to resolve the two bandits' differences. For as soon as visitors returned to Vallecito, so too were sightings of their ghosts reported.

They were seen most often by those camped close to Vallecito Station. Witnesses claimed to hear the footsteps from their tents: the sound of a man in boots and spurs walking in the adobe building. Many of those who went out to investigate claimed that they saw a man with a wide-brimmed hat on his head walking out of the station before vanishing in thin air. And sure enough, witnesses brave enough to investigate after having laid eyes on this disappearing bandit have seen the shimmering image of luckless Bill lying face down in the same corner he was shot.

While most sightings of these long-dead outlaws occur within the station, a few campers claimed to have heard the jangling spurs outside. The campsites closest to the station have been rich ground for paranormal phenomena. Over the years, many campers at these sites have heard the sound of the phantom outlaw's footsteps walking through their campsites. Many have lain in terrified silence throughout the night, too frightened to move, convinced that someone was standing just outside. Those able to gather enough courage to confront the presence outside have emerged from their tents to the sight of the empty night.

Has the ghost of the dead bandit finally managed to leave the building where he was shot dead? Does his spirit remain behind in the hope of finding his buried treasure? Or could this lonely ghost be looking for some sort of company in the desert night? Who knows, perhaps he finds it. For there is one other famous ghost in that oasis: the White Lady of Vallecito.

2
Wandering Women

One More Tragedy in Vallecito

She comes with the twilight, a luminous apparition of a woman in a resplendent white gown, rising from her unmarked grave behind the adobe building and floating to the front entrance, where she remains for several moments before vanishing into the air. She is the White Lady of Vallecito, a famous phantom that has haunted the old station since she died there over 150 years ago.

Her name was Eileen O'Connor, a young woman from the East who was making her way to Sacramento to marry her beau, a gold prospector who had just struck it rich in the California gold fields. She booked passage on the Butterfield Line and began the journey with joyful expectation, but somewhere along the way, Eileen fell ill. By the time her coach arrived at the Vallecito Station she was too weak to continue. Her fellow passengers carried her to the bed in the back of the station, where she was tended to by the station employees. They did all they could, but it was soon evident that she was beyond any help. The third day after she arrived, O'Connor succumbed to her fever.

She had been delirious during her final days, and the people taking care of her learned little about who she was. They went through her possessions looking for information about her identity, but all she was carrying was a satin wedding dress and a locket containing a photograph of her beau. No one knew who the man in the locket was, let alone how to contact him, so they dressed Eileen in her wedding gown and buried her in an anonymous grave behind the station. When her loved ones eventually discovered what had happened, none of them had the heart to have her remains exhumed, and she remained in her lonely plot behind station, far from friends and family and home.

Eileen O'Connor did not rest peacefully. Sightings of the White Lady of Vallecito began soon after she was interred. No one can say exactly when she rose from the grave for the first time, but it was said to be during a spectacular sunset sometime in 1859. She rose under a blood red sky, her pale face completely expressionless except for a deep sadness that emanated from her eyes. Glowing faintly in the darkening desert, her transparent apparition drifted over the dirt to the front of the station. Several witnesses stared in utter silence as the White Lady stood there, waiting, it seemed, for something to arrive. She hovered there for a few minutes before she began to fade. And then she was gone, leaving nothing but a dry wind and a haunting sadness behind her.

It was the first of countless appearances. The White Lady was seen by numerous passengers of the Butterfield Line until 1861, when the company abandoned Vallecito Station. It's impossible to know whether or not she continued to appear in front of the station during its long period of abandonment, but as soon as people began visiting again when it was made a park in the 1930s, stories of the White Lady began to circulate once more. Is her spirit, unable to cope with the tragedy of her death, waiting for a carriage to take her to her beau? If so, it is fitting that she keeps company with the bandit ghosts of Vallecito, who, like the spirit of Eileen O'Connor, met their end before they could claim their treasure.

The Ghost of Poor Old Eilley Bowers

Allison "Eilley" Oram was the grande dame of early Nevada. An early settler in the Washoe Valley, she was one of the extraordinary women of western America, winning and losing her fortune by the tumultuous boom and bust conditions of the mining frontier. Born in Scotland on September 6, 1826, Eilley married when she was 15 and moved to the Great Salt Lake soon after with Stephen Hunter, her devoutly Mormon husband. It would be the last time she would ride on the coattails of any man.

In a time when divorce was not a realistic option for so many women, young Eilley left her husband after they arrived in America; the reasons behind this separation are forgotten by history, but whatever they were, they did not spoil the idea of marriage for the Scot. She married another Mormon named Alexander Cowan in 1853. Two years later, man and wife moved to what is now Nevada. Acting as Mormon missionaries, the two set up a ranch near present-day Genoa, moving on to the Washoe Valley in western Nevada about one year later. Although Eilley was already an anomaly among women in her willingness to settle on the rough fringes of American civilization, she became one of the legendary figures of the region when she decided to stay behind in the Washoe Valley after her husband was called back to Utah by the Mormon order.

She effectively ended her marriage to Alexander Cowan, and it was not long before she was rewarded for her bold independence. Moving south to a small mining camp called

Johntown, she set up a boarding house, supplying miners with decent rooms in a rough settlement where tents were the dominant shelter. The move was fortuitous. In 1859 gold was discovered on a nearby hill, and miners rushed into the region, bringing a suddenly booming business to the enterprising young woman. She was not content to live off the earnings of the miners, however, and quickly got involved in the mining herself. Because she lived in the region before the rush of miners began, Eilley had her pick of the mining plots along Gold Hill. One of her claims bordered on another claim owned by one Lemuel "Sandy" Bowers. The handsome young Scotsman developed a deep admiration for Eilley's dauntless ambition, and the two were wed under fortunate auspices, as both their claims began churning out incredible amounts of wealth.

Eilley and Sandy Bowers became Nevada's first two millionaires. Tapping into the enormous Comstock Lode, the couple became the recipients of more money than they had ever dared to imagine. This abundance of cash greased the wheels of their nuptial arrangements, and a true and lasting love formed between them. But with greater wealth came greater potential for tragedy. The more one has, the more one has to lose. Fortune's familiar pattern of generous bestowal and cruel deprivation did not spare the Bowerses. The twists of fate Eilley would suffer throughout the rest of her days turned her attention to mystical forces, and she spent the last years of her life looking to the spirits of the underworld for guidance.

The Bowerses' impending misfortunes arrived along with their first two children, who both died in infancy. Perhaps the Bowerses were seeking some respite from the sorrow of these losses when they commissioned their mansion to be built and took off on a 10-month trip through Europe. They came back to their newly constructed mansion along with a child they had adopted somewhere in the Scottish highlands; Eilley was never forthcoming about the girl's background.

But the Bowerses would not have too much time to enjoy any familial happiness. Soon after they returned, their mines began to run out. Outstanding debts suddenly loomed large before the young family, and their savings and income rapidly deteriorated. By the time Sandy went to their mines on Gold Hill to oversee the operation, the ore had all but run out. Poverty, however, was not an issue Mr. Bowers had to contend with for too long. With a broken heart and lungs full of rock dust, Sandy died of silicosis early in 1868.

Eilley was alone once again, doing everything she could to raise her adopted daughter in a world that was decidedly hostile to independent women. She turned her mansion into a boarding house in hopes of paying off her debts, but her efforts were in vain. She became more removed from reality as her fortunes plummeted, yet it was in 1874, when her daughter died after her appendix burst in a Reno boarding school, that Eilley's worldview changed dramatically.

She lost her mansion in a public auction in 1876 and spent the rest of her life dabbling in the spirit world, making a meager living looking into her crystal ball, giving superstitious clients a look into their futures for a small price. She also claimed she could communicate with spirits of the departed, and charged a fee to deliver messages to clients' deceased loved ones. After wandering between California and Nevada, the once incredibly wealthy mine proprietor's last days were spent in an Oakland, California, poorhouse. She died on October 27, 1903.

But that would not be the last the world would hear of Eilley Bowers. Strange things began to happen in the Bowers Mansion soon after she passed away. There were reports of mysterious sounds coming from deserted hallways and rooms. People described them as shuffling sounds; objects were being moved about, as if someone was looking for a missing possession, emptying closets, nightstands and dressers. But investigations never revealed any intruder, just an empty, rearranged chamber.

Other people claimed to see a stately looking matriarch dressed in Victorian splendor standing stoically before one of the mansion's windows, looking out on the estate's sprawling grounds. The woman was described as broad, with short dark hair and hard features, descriptions that match the portraits of the same legendary entrepreneur who had the mansion built.

These sightings have increased dramatically since the Bowers Mansion was opened for tours. Many believe Eilley is returning for her crystal ball, which is displayed in the mansion today. Others think that her spirit is reliving those few days of happiness when she was living in the mansion with her daughter and husband, before the cruel hands of fate tore their household apart.

La Posada Hotel

Fortune was not kind to Julia Schuster, whose life changed the moment she caught the eye of Abraham Staab, a Santa Fe magnate visiting his German homeland on a nuptial quest. In the 19th century, the rules of courtship were different than they are today. The worth of a woman was measured by the status of her husband, and Abraham Staab was a powerful millionaire who made sure he got what he wanted. Julia really didn't have much of a choice; an offer of marriage from a man as powerful as Staab was not to be turned down. Shortly after she was wed, Julia moved to Santa Fe with her new husband.

It was 1876, a time when the New Mexico town was on the peripheries of civilization. Julia spent the remainder her life there, far away from her homeland and everyone she loved, contending with one heart-rending difficulty after another until death claimed her in 1896. She spent her final years dying slowly and painfully, ensconced within the luxurious space of her bedroom in the Staab Mansion, a true victim of the genteel mores she was taught to live by.

Abraham could not know he was commissioning the construction of his wife's tomb when he ordered work to begin on the opulent three-story Staab Mansion in 1884. Making sure he made up in material splendor everything he lacked in emotional depth, Abraham insisted his house be made into one of the most magnificent homes in Santa Fe. The Victorian-era mansion was filled with every luxury that money could buy, and Abraham and his wife entertained the socialites of New Mexico with some of the finest parties in the Southwest.

But a debilitating unhappiness rested underneath the velvet veneer of Victorian opulence. Abraham Staab was a hard man whose connection with his family rested primarily on incessant, often vicious demands that he get his way. He insisted that his wife act according to his perceptions of propriety, that he should have as many children as he wished and that all his children fulfill familial obligations, meaning unconditional obedience to their father. For Julia, who gave birth to four boys and four girls, this meant decades of ceaseless work and emotional isolation. Expected to maintain an image of upper-class gentility, Julia learned to keep her complaints to herself, languishing in her own loneliness until a deep sadness settled on her soul.

Yet it was after one of her sons died in infancy that something inside Julia snapped. Not long after that, she fell victim to what history only describes as a "dreadful accident," emerging with an unnamed physical disability that kept her confined to her bedroom. An invalid for the rest of her life, she spent the remainder of her days festering in an ugly depression, seen by no one, not even her husband, until she died. While it is widely accepted that she died of illness, many have whispered rumors of homicide, and there has been more than one story of Abraham Staab stealing into Julia's room while she was sleeping to smother her with a pillow or shoot her with a pistol.

Many state that such rumors grew from the imaginations of those community members who tend to assume the worst, that Abraham Staab went through great pains to assure his wife got the best medical treatment, and would never have committed such an act. Whatever the case, as meek as Julia Staab was when she was alive, suffering so many years of

The adobe interior of La Posada Hotel

physical and emotional pain in stoic silence, subsequent events at the Staab Mansion suggest that she has not crossed over to the afterlife with the same docility.

In 1934, years after both Julia and Abraham had passed away, R.H. and Eulalia Nason, a wealthy couple from the Midwest, moved to Santa Fe on the recommendation of their doctor, who swore by the health benefits of the New Mexico climate. The Nasons were bewitched by the local culture and joined the Pueblo Revival Movement shortly after they purchased the Staab property. It was under their auspices that the current La Posada Resort and Spa was established. The adobes built around the Victorian mansion were eventually used as the lavish suites on the sprawling grounds of the luxurious resort that anyone can visit in Santa Fe today.

The Staab Mansion still stands in the center of the resort, housing a restaurant, bar and a number of ornate suites on the second floor. And it is there, in room 256, that the ghost of Julia Staab is believed to reside. It is the same room where she spent the last years of her life suffering in a solitary bedridden misery. Guests have reported waking in the middle of the night to see a well-dressed, slightly transparent woman standing over their beds, or walking about the room randomly moving their belongings about. Whenever this woman is addressed, she vanishes into thin air before their eyes.

Other guests in room 256 have come back to their rooms after a day of sight seeing in Santa Fe to find their belongings rearranged. Suitcases that were open were found closed, toiletries that were in the bathroom were arranged meticulously atop the nightstand in the bedroom and towels previously folded on towel racks were spread over the floor in careful patterns.

There is also the time Julia turned up the heat during one of Santa Fe's cold spells. It happened one evening when the temperature in Santa Fe suddenly and unexpectedly dropped, leaving the residents in La Posada shivering in their rooms. The story goes that the only person who had the key to operate the thermostat had gone fishing, and the clerk at the front desk was being flooded with calls about the cold in their rooms. Sometime between seven and eight o'clock, a call came in from room 256. A woman with a thick German accent told the clerk what he had already heard a dozen times that evening, except for adding that her guests were all half-frozen. When he answered the best he could do was provide some blankets and hot beverages until the maintenance man with the thermostat key arrived, he received a brisk response: "Neveer, mind, I vill take care of eet myself."

Moments later, the heater was running, and within the hour the hotel was a comfortable room temperature. The man finished his shift not thinking much of the heater, assuming that the maintenance man had returned and turned it back on. The clerk ran into the caretaker on his way out of the hotel, and thanked him for turning the heat on. "Pardon me?" the caretaker replied, "I just got back in now. I didn't turn the heat on."

The strange call from room 256 instantly replayed itself in the clerk's mind. What did she mean by "her guests" being half-frozen? And he didn't recall anyone staying in room 256 having a German accent.

Julia continues to haunt La Posada today, appearing repeatedly to guests staying in her room. She has also been spotted drifting down the second floor hallway, a pale woman dressed in 19th-century finery. She keeps a careful eye on the guests in her home, doing everything she can to ensure that guests in La Posada are enjoying their stay.

The Legend of La Llorona

Anyone who knows their Hispanic folklore might wonder if the world really needs another account of the legend of La Llorona (pronounced lah-yoh-roh-nah in Spanish). Said to have been around for over 500 years, the narrative of the Weeping Woman has been told and retold countless times all across Latin America, from the southern tip of Argentina to the banks of the Rio Grande and into parts of Arizona, New Mexico, Texas and California. Why, then, repeat this legend about a beautiful young woman and a single act of desperate madness?

Well, simply because it won't go away. Old as it is, the story continues to circulate. It finds new life with every whispered telling from parent to child, after each time teenagers parked on Arizona riverbanks are interrupted by a high-pitched wail or whenever campers spot a tall, luminescent woman all in white hovering on the edge of some New Mexico lake. Incredible as it seems, the legend of La Llorona survives to this day, and so it is being included in this collection of supernatural stories from the American Southwest.

Not that it's an easy story to tell. There are many widely varying versions, but they do have some basic elements in common—they all involve a strikingly attractive young woman, an ill-conceived affair with some callous man, a brutal act of infanticide, and then the sightings of the woman's tortured spirit, unable to come to terms with the act she has committed.

Sometimes her name is María, sometimes Louisa, other times Malinche. In one popular version she is an Aztec woman who has had the ill fortune of falling for a heartless

Spanish conquistador; in other versions she is a beautiful village girl of humble origins who gets involved with a rakish womanizer, a rich ranchero or a handsome traveler. But in other variations she is a vain and selfish woman, intent on doing anything to hold on to her lover. The end result, though, is always the same.

What follows is one of the more popular versions:

She was born in a humble little Mexican pueblo, and while she was alive, broke the heart of every man who lived there. The luster of her shining black hair and the dark and perfect symmetry of her beautiful face caused every man who saw her to fall for her. And it wasn't her looks alone. She was also imbued with an extraordinary grace, her gentle and refined mannerisms making her something of an outsider in the rough town that was her home. Eyes followed her whenever she walked down the street, and the townsfolk wondered how one of the poorest families in such a poor town could produce such a regal beauty.

Coveted as she was by every man in the village, such fervent admiration only served to isolate her. Every man wanted her, but no man felt worthy of her, and so it was that this young woman's beauty perpetually set apart from the rest of the townsfolk. It was agreed by everyone that no one in this lowly town of dirt farmers and poor ranchers deserved such extraordinary beauty.

Then an adventurer from Mexico City rode into town on a summer's night, wandering the countryside just for the sake of it. He was a big man on a big horse with a ready laugh and enough money to buy the town, and minutes after he strode into the pueblo's only bar, he had won the esteem of the local sporting men.

It was a rare thing for the men of this town to play host to a man of such obvious means. He spent his money without issue, buying rounds for everyone in the bar each time he ordered for himself and losing hand after hand of cards with happy nonchalance, laughing and telling stories of strange places that none of them had seen. In the bar that night, tequila, mirth and laughter were in no short supply. With the help of his bottomless wallet and his copious losses at the gambling tables, the stranger lit up the establishment.

The party went on until the first trace of morning light broke the darkness. The stranger grew suddenly serious. He looked around the dark bar, then, and spoke: "Thank you, my friends," he said, slurring through the tequila, "you have shown a lone wanderer great hospitality, but the sun has come up now and it's time for me to go. The horizon calls."

"No!" came the drunken shout from the tavern. One man staggered to his feet, saying, "Will you forget this night's brotherhood? You are welcome here, to our town and its treasures, as though it were your home."

"Its treasures?" the stranger said with a smile. "Besides the friendship of gallant men such as yourselves, what kind of treasures do you suppose your town might offer?"

"We have a woman here," the man replied, "a woman whose beauty defies every man in this village. I promise you that though you may wander all over this country and the world beyond, you will never see such a beauty as the one that dwells here with us." Shouts of agreement sounded in the bar. All the men were thinking of the woman who had haunted their dreams, and knew that the stranger would likewise be smitten with his first look. And unlike every other man in the room, this stranger, they knew, with his great wealth and gregarious manner, would not allow himself to be tortured by such a thing as beauty. He would act. Here, they said to themselves, was someone who was worthy of her.

"A woman?" the stranger asked, his interest visibly piqued. It had been a while since he had enjoyed such company. Many señoritas admired him, yes, but he wasn't the type of man to become entangled with such things. With his lofty pedigree, great wealth and irrepressible wanderlust, he was in no rush to pick a wife. The road still called to him, and in all his travels he had yet to encounter a woman who could cause him to reconsider his rootless ways. Nevertheless, he had enjoyed himself in this town, and was amused at the thought of marching to a woman's home at this hour with such a band of drunks. "Believe me, amigos, I've seen quite a few beautiful señoritas in my day," he finally said with a laugh, "but because you've been such splendid hosts, I will agree to visit this woman you speak of."

And so it was that every man in the bar rose to take the stranger to the woman they adored. For his part, the wanderer took a few minutes to ready himself, shaving his face, twirling his grand mustache into two fine points and brushing the dust off his sombrero and riding clothes. When he was done, he fell in with his retinue of gamblers, who promptly spilled out onto the street, singing and shouting all the way to the humble home of the town's most celebrated woman.

The sun had risen and the roosters were crowing when the crowd arrived. The woman's father was already awake, working on the fence in his front yard. For years, the old man had been painfully aware of how coveted his daughter was. He had spent much of the last few years chasing stricken young men with their anonymous love letters from his door. He was forced to cut down the tree in the yard that provided a view into his daughter's bedroom. And when his daughter had complained that she was often woken in the night by amorous whispers from men hiding under her window, he sealed it with shutters that could not be opened. Indeed, when the drunken mob of men arrived, he had been making his fence higher in an attempt to put an end to the obscene letters that were nightly deposited at his doorstep, not knowing that he would not have to worry about the lovelorn and lustful for too much longer.

He stopped his hammering and looked at the drunken congregation with open hostility. *Has the time finally come?* he thought to himself. Had the riffraff he had contended with for so long finally decided enough was enough? Were they here to take his daughter away? He stepped out to meet them, scowling, hammer in hand. "What are you doing here at such an early hour, making such a racket and reeking of tequila?"

The man who had spoken to the stranger earlier stepped forward and cleared his throat. "We are here, señor," inflating his voice to absurd proportions, "because a great visitor from abroad has arrived, seeking audience with your daughter."

The father's scowl deepened; he tightened his grip on his hammer. "A great visitor from abroad?" he said. "Where is this great visitor? I see nothing but drunken fools before me."

At this, the stranger straightened and stepped forward, an amused grin on his face. "Forgive me, señor, I should have announced myself. I arrived in your fine town last evening, and have greatly enjoyed the hospitality of these fine friends." A little cheer went up from the drunks. "This morning, I was about to go on my way, when I was told that this was not a possibility without looking at least once upon the treasure of the town. I have been told that your daughter is finest among all women, and I would be a fool to leave without meeting her."

The father was silent, unsure of what to make of this man standing before him. He was drunk, certainly, but it was obvious by his bearing and the quality of his clothes that he was a man of means. The woman's father was not so quick to rebuke this visitor, not only because he was obviously wealthy, but also because he desperately wanted to see his daughter married. He had grown tired of defending her honor from all the bumbling fools in town, all of whom were cowed by his daughter's beauty. He looked at this stranger and thought, *Here, at last, is someone who may be worthy of her.*

So it was that drunken admirers and protective father were thinking along the same lines when the woman herself appeared on the road. She had gone to fetch water from the well and was returning with a full jug on her hip. Her dress was threadbare and patched in places, the hem covered with the dirt of the road.

She had been smiling, but her expression dropped upon taking in the sight of the men crowded around her house, each of them looking at her with that mix of unfathomable hope and impossible expectation that she had long grown accustomed to seeing in the eyes of men. Holding her head high and continuing to her home, she did not take notice of the stranger among them, standing a hand or two taller than the rest, with his finely combed mustache, fancy riding clothes and enormous sombrero.

But he noticed her. Indeed, the moment she crested the hill, he ceased noting anything else. *By God, they were right!* the man thought as he stood agape, unable to believe his eyes. *She is the most beautiful woman that I've ever seen!* And all at once, he knew he had to have her. He would do any-thing: settle down; give up all his money; even live in this town, with these drunken simpletons as his neighbors.

"Father?" the girl said upon reaching the gate. He was looking at her in a way he never had before.

"There is someone I would like you to meet," the father said to his daughter. "He has come from many miles to meet you."

At this, the stranger took off his sombrero and stepped forward. He had never been the sort of man to lose his com-posure, but standing face to face with this woman, he found himself unable to form a single thought. Suddenly terrified that in his wide-eyed silence he might appear indistinguish-able from the pitiful mob crowded behind him, the stranger forced words to his mouth.

"Señorita," he said, moving closer, "let me take this water from you, it looks like a difficult burden to carry."

And with these simple words, the young woman fell in love. Was it the way he spoke, his formal language setting him apart from the men she had always known? Could it have been that he wore the finest riding clothes she had ever seen? The enormous sombrero tucked under his arm? His lavish mustache? Or perhaps it might have had something to do with the fact that he had just looked her in the face and managed to say something, which was more than any man besides her father had been able to accomplish since she had been a child. Whatever it was, she decided then and there that she loved this man.

So began a short courting period, which led to marriage, a home and, in less than two years' time, two children—a baby boy and a baby girl. Yet things were not well in their house. Indeed, their happiness began to crumble not long after they made their vows. Although the young woman's beauty was awe-inspiring, it turned out that it wasn't enough to completely kill the stranger's wanderlust. After all, he had stopped by the town for a night of cards and tequila, and the next time he had a chance to look around, he had built a home for a wife and children he had somehow acquired. The local men were good for one night of inebriation, but it didn't take long for him to grow sick to death of every last one of them. He had barely been married for half a year before he began taking longer and longer trips away from home, inventing any reason he could think of to get away from the tiny town that had accidentally become his home. And his beautiful wife accompanied him on almost none of these excursions.

The stranger was the first to admit that there were few women as fair as his wife, but soon after he was married, he also came to realize that there were more important things than mere beauty. He was from a noble family of considerable wealth, well educated and used to a certain worldliness in his companions. His wife, on the other hand, was a simple girl who had never been outside her village. The man never looked at her the same way after he realized that her company was scarcely better than that of the men at the bar.

It did not take long after this realization for their marriage to start falling apart. His trips away from town began to grow longer and longer, and when he was in town, it was obvious that his mind was elsewhere. He could barely be bothered with his wife's concerns, and found it evermore difficult to contain his frustration with her provincial ways. But no matter what foolishness came out of her mouth, he was never completely unaffected by her beauty, and was never overtly offensive to her. The children, however, were another story.

Perhaps because it was impossible for him to vent his frustrations on his wife, his children bore the brunt of all the misgivings he had about his marriage. He took to hollering at the youngsters if they made so much as a peep. He never looked them in the eye, and did not so much as touch either of them. More than once, he stormed out of the house in the middle of the night on account of their crying, sometimes not returning for weeks.

No one knows how his wife reacted to such slights during this period. She certainly could not have been happy, but even if she was absolutely miserable, the social conventions of her time would not allow her to leave her husband. Such conventions, however, did not exist for men, and her husband ended up leaving her.

She did not even know that their marriage was over until the day she saw him with another woman. She was surprised at first when she saw him pull up in a carriage in front of the town's general store. Her husband had always preferred to ride on horseback, and this was the first time he had come to town in a carriage. But everything was made abundantly clear when he emerged from the carriage with a resplendently dressed woman on his arm. Catching sight of his wife and children at the end of the street, he immediately gave the woman he was with a long kiss. His wife stormed down the street and began shouting, using every word for two-faced liar that she had in her vocabulary, but he just looked at her dumbly. "Certainly, señora, you do not mean to say that we are acquainted," he said, looking from his wife to the two children in her arms. "I have never been in this village before, and let me assure you, I would never bring up children here. Now good bye."

The woman lost her mind. She ran home, wailing at the top of her voice the entire way. She remained locked in her house for weeks, refusing to see anyone, not even her mother or father. Isolating herself in her misery, the townsfolk could only guess at what was going on behind those closed doors. No one in town could have known how bad it had gotten for her—until it was too late.

The last time anyone saw her, it was evening, and a violent summer storm was raging. She was seen moving fast down the town's main street, clothed in a long white dress, soaked to the skin, her two children in her arms. Those who saw her only caught the split-second glimpses illuminated by lightning flashes. Her dark hair was plastered to her face, which was bent into an expression of utter madness. By her look, it wasn't clear whether she was weeping or laughing, but the blood-chilling wail that sounded down the street made it clear enough. Grief had consumed her.

The rain was falling so hard that the river nearby had become a rushing torrent, very nearly flowing over its banks. There was one man who saw it happen—he followed her to the riverbank and watched in horror as she raised her children, one at a time, over her head and hurled them with all her might into the river below. The man was shocked as the

Sometimes she just stood and stared out on the water.

raving young mother's frenzied hysteria dissolved into manic grief right before his eyes. Realizing the enormity of what she had just done, she fell to her knees and let out a terrible cry that carried above the storm and all through the town. "Ay! Ayeeeeeeeeeee! My babies!" With this, she threw herself into the roaring river, casting her life away in those powerful currents, her body never to be found.

But, of course, this is only the beginning of the age-old legend of La Llorona. For it was not long after this night that whispered sightings of a deathly pale woman in a long white dress with sleek black hair began to circulate around the town. She was usually seen at night, shimmering and semi-transparent, her once-beautiful features gaunt and desiccated, her once-lively brown eyes sunken into twin pits. Sometimes she just stood and stared out on the water; on other occasions, witnesses claimed she raised her head to the stars and wailed the same way she did the night she threw her children into the river.

Terrifying as these encounters were, no adult who saw her on the banks of the river ever came to any harm; however, it was a completely different matter for any children who had the misfortune of stumbling on La Llorona at night. There is no sure story about the first child that vanished on the banks of the river, but over the years, it became accepted among the children of the town that to stay out too late on the banks of the river was to risk their lives. Ever on the search for her own children, La Llorona would settle for others foolish enough to venture near the river after dark, where the woman in white would drag them into the cold black depths.

Somehow, countless versions of this legend spread all across Latin America, though the details of the story were hardly consistent. Sometimes La Llorona was not the victim of a highborn wanderer, but a selfish beauty who drowned her children from a previous marriage so that she could marry a new love interest. In this telling, she is overcome by guilt and ends up committing suicide. In other versions, it is her father who commits the crime, killing the children of his widowed daughter so that she will be able to marry a wealthy young man who has taken an interest in her. If the story is set in a coastal town, she loses her children in the ocean. If she lives near a lake, that is where her children drown. She is always a beautiful young woman, she is always coupled with a man of a higher social station, and her children always die, but the details of La Llorona's story are wide open.

Yet despite such inconsistency, the legend continues to survive. Today, all across Arizona and New Mexico, all sorts of tales are being told about La Llorona. She is abducting children, taking them down to murky depths in any south-western body of water. She is keeping others awake, her coyote-like cry for her long lost children breaking the night's silence. Sometimes she is a moral force, appearing to frighten rebellious teenagers into listening to their parents. In other stories she is even a harbinger of good fortune. These versions tell us of the pale woman in a white dress with black hair appearing before poor farmers, hovering over an area that contained buried treasure. An evil spirit that steals children? A disciplining ghost that assists parents in keeping their teenagers in line? A kind soul concerned with the poverty of Latin American farmers? La Llorona seems to be all of these things, depending on when and where one hears her tale.

3
Indian Legends

The Evil at Urraca Mesa

Philmont Scout Ranch requires little introduction to anyone who is or ever was associated with the Boy Scouts of America. A 287,000-acre wilderness preserve located in northeastern New Mexico, Philmont is the yearly destination of some 20,000 scouts who, every summer, arrive from all corners of the country. There, rigorous hikes take them through forests and meadows, across tumbling rivers and over rocky peaks to some of the grandest outdoor vistas the United States has to offer.

And yet as beautiful as the Philmont Ranch is, there is also a mystery to the wilderness there—an ancient foreboding in every root, branch, mountaintop and stream, which haunted the land long before eager Boy Scouts went marching through it. Indeed, the darkness that lurks there predates the railroad, the pioneers, the first wave of fortune seekers, even the Ute, Kiowa, Comanche and Apache tribes that roamed there. Perhaps the evil is as old as the land itself.

The first people to settle the area that is now New Mexico, a tribe called the Anasazi, arrived thousands of years before anyone else. What little is known of them comes to us by archeological study. A technologically primitive people, they lived and they died there for many generations. Then, around 900 years ago, they were wiped out. It isn't clear today exactly what happened. What is known is that the Anasazi demise was swift and brutal, caused by lethal violence on a massive scale. Often grisly evidence indicates death by torture. Were they invaded by another tribe? Did they turn on one another?

No one knows. But when the Navajo settled the area next, they discovered the remains of those who had been before. And it was there, amid the dead relics, that they sensed something else. There was evil there. Evil spirits from another place haunted the waters, the trees, the stones. There were demons in the air that needed to be harnessed, lest the Navajo, too, suffer the same fate as the Anasazi. The Navajo shamans came to know that this evil was concentrated atop Urraca Mesa, which they said was a gateway to a demon world.

And so it was that these shamans, the most feared and respected of their people, erected four ceremonial cat totems atop the mesa, sealing the gateway shut. The totems ensured that the evil denizens from beneath would not be able to come to the world, and one shaman, the wisest and most powerful among them, was given the sacred duty of watching over the holy totems, guarding them from nature and human intruders alike. As long as at least one of the totems stood, the demons would be kept from the earth.

Yet the Navajo would not shoulder the terrible responsibility of Urraca Mesa for very long. A rival band, the fierce Jicarilla Apache, was approaching, and none of the Navajo were too eager to fight for a land blighted by the shadow of the looming Urraca Mesa. When the Apache arrived, they too recognized the evil of the mesa, and not even their bravest warriors dared to ascend its heights.

The Spaniards came next, encased in cuirasses, bringing bloodshed on halberds and the tips of their swords, followed by the first wave of English-speaking adventurers from the East. The arrival of colonizers ushered in a new era. The region was flooded with pale-skinned settlers and eventually passed from Spain to Mexico, and then, after the Mexican-American War of 1846, to the United States. The violence did not subside after the war. It mattered not to the local Indians what distant power claimed lordship over them, and hostile Comanches, Kiowas, Apaches and Utes waged constant battle against the American outsiders who came flooding into their lands. In the tumultuous decades that followed, Urraca Mesa and the evil said to reside within was all but forgotten. Those white settlers who heard the story would have likely dismissed it as primitive superstition, while the Indians themselves were facing dangers far greater and more immediate in the swarms of blue-coat soldiers fighting to herd them into reservations. Thus, in the face of the momentous events of 1840s on, the story of the demons atop Urraca Mesa were largely disregarded, a half-remembered native tale amid countless others, of interest only to folklorists and those interested in the culture of the Southwest. Not that the Indians ever completely forgot.

The legend continued to be passed on over succeeding generations. By the time the Philmont Ranch was deeded to the Boy Scouts in 1941, the two remaining cat totems on top of Urraca Mesa—time has claimed the other two—were well entrenched in the canon of local folklore. But as the Boy Scouts started taking their regular expeditions over the mesa, a number of hikers began to sense that there was indeed something strange and unsettling about the elevated plateau that rose above Philmont Ranch. It started with vague impressions among certain scouts, and as the years passed and more and more boys clambered up Urraca Mesa's slopes, weird accounts began to surface—of eerie forces, powerful

Urraca Mesa was believed by Navajo shamans to be a gateway to a demon world.

and unseen, that tormented lone hikers, of inexplicable apparitions and strange sounds.

The fact that on topographic maps the top of Urraca Mesa forms the profile of a human skull has done nothing to quell the stories. So Urraca Mesa has taken its place in Boy Scout lore, and the ancient evil that concerned the Navajo so much has returned, this time to chill the spines of ranch employees as well as intrepid Boy Scouts on their summer holidays.

Certainly, more than one person spending the night at Urraca Camp will attest to the fact that strange things are afoot. Located among trees at the base of the mesa, the scenic campsite borders an expansive meadow. Although the camp is actually a good hike from the peak of the mesa, it is apparently still close enough to attract the attention of the forces that reside there.

The following account was provided by author and outdoor enthusiast Michael Connelly, in his work *Riders in the Sky: The Ghosts and Legends of Philmont Scout Ranch.* Connelly's witness is Ron Walker, a camp director who was just starting his third year at Philmont Ranch in the summer of 1997. The hour was late, and Walker had just settled down for bed when four loud knocks sounded on his cabin door. Assuming that a ranch employee or camper was in need of some kind of assistance, Walker pulled himself out of his bunk. Yet when he opened the door, no one was there. He took a step out and looked down the porch, which ran the length of the cabin. No one.

Walker didn't need to deliberate long to come to the conclusion that camp pranksters were at work. He stepped back in the cabin and shut the door, intent on waiting right beside it so that he would catch the culprits in the act when they knocked again, which he was certain they would. Sure enough, he didn't have to wait for long. The second round of knocks came less than a minute later. This time, Walker was ready, throwing open the door an instant after the last rap.

A sudden uncertainty flooded in with the moonlight. Nobody was there. He stepped out onto the porch and took another look. Not a soul. *Impossible,* Walker thought, *there was no way anyone could vanish that fast.* He'd opened the door mere seconds after the knocking had stopped. There was a full moon out, and silver light shone over the wide meadow in front of the cabin. He would easily be able to see the culprits running in that direction, and as for the porch— it was simply not possible for anyone to have crossed it in the time that it took him to open the door, and without making a single sound, no less. Stepping back into the cabin, Walker wasn't given a moment to think before four heavy knocks rapped on the cabin's back wall. He hadn't taken a step toward the window when the same staccato pounding sounded on another wall.

Then it began—four knocks on each wall, circling around the house, slowly at first, then faster and faster, reaching an inhuman speed, as though the cabin was surrounded by dozens of people knocking in a flawless pattern. But that wasn't it. In a matter of seconds, the knocking had grown so fast and forceful that the house had become a pounding cacophony, its walls shaking under whatever unnatural force had beset it.

Walker's hands instinctively went to his ears, and he stumbled backward into his bedroom, sliding to the floor, trying to control the panic that was welling up inside of him.

While hiking up the slopes of Urraca Mesa, many Boy Scouts have encountered inexplicable apparitions and strange sounds.

In his narration of the event, Michael Connelly doesn't say how long the pounding went on, but it continued until Walker finally found his voice. Hardly thinking straight, the camp director shouted out the first two words that came to mind, hollering, "Thank you!" at the top of his voice.

The knocking stopped then, so suddenly that the ensuing silence seemed just as loud. Walker was obviously someone who was familiar with the story of Urraca Mesa, because according to Connelly, the first thing that came to mind as he sat there in that absolute and utter silence was the Navajo legend of the ancient evil and the four cat totems and the shaman who was left behind to guard them.

"He realized why the phrase he had yelled had had such an immediate effect," Connelly writes. "The knocking was the signal of the old Navajo shaman, assigned centuries ago to protect the cat totems on the mesa. The rapping was a rhythm of four beats repeated over and over again, a noisy, but effective notification by the shaman's spirit that he is still on the job."

Some might think it odd that the director would automatically equate the knocking with the spirit of a long-dead shaman. But Walker, like so many familiar with the region, would have known the legend of Urraca Mesa. Furthermore, he would have heard of all the weird things that were said to go on atop the skull-shaped plateau.

Over the years, the testaments have been many. There are those who have spoken of a big ball of blue light floating over the mesa, hovering at a distance, filling observers with an undeniable sense that, somehow, it is watching them. Most people promptly back away, but there are others who have approached it. Apparently, such bravery is rewarded with a sighting of the shaman himself, standing silent in the center of the blue orb. He appears as an elderly man with braided gray hair and deep wrinkles that frame watchful, intelligent eyes. He's adorned in the ceremonial trappings of a Navajo shaman, with ornamented buckskin leggings, shirt and a majestic headdress crowned with buffalo horns. It is also widely believed that during the day, he maintains his vigil in an alternate form, appearing as a massive panther, bear or wolf, watching hikers carefully from a distance.

Thus the shaman still keeps his guard over the cat totems on the mesa. Originally there were four of these ceremonial markers, which is why Walker instantly thought that it was the spirit of the shaman that was knocking on his cabin— four knocks on each wall—just to let the camp director know of his presence.

But why come all the way down from the top of the mesa? Of course, it is impossible to say, and any explanation is pure speculation, but there are theories that the spirit of the lone shaman has gotten more aggressive as the cat totems have fallen. With only two remaining, the spirit is making it clear that he will brook no mischief where the Navajo relics are concerned. He's still there, he wants all to know, and as long as he is, nothing will happen to the cat totems. Considering what happened to the Anasazi in the region so many years ago, perhaps we should consider ourselves lucky that the Navajo gave the charge to such a diligent soul.

The Angry Phantom
and the Boy Scout

There's reason to believe that the shaman isn't the only spirit on Urraca Mesa—and that, perhaps, the lone Navajo holy man hasn't been entirely successful keeping the evil ones on their side of the gateway. For despite the shaman's numerous appearances, there is reason to believe that there are other spirits atop the mesa, ones that are known to be far more interactive with hikers. Pretty well none of those hikers who have had run-ins with these spirits are too thrilled about this fact. Certainly Ben James was not.

Ben James, another scout interviewed by Michael Connelly in *Riders in the Sky*, was enrolled in the United States Naval Academy in 1990, the year he had his close encounter with the thing on Urraca Mesa. His summer assignment was to work as a ranger at Philmont Ranch, prepping greenhorn hikers for their 11-day expeditions through the mountains. He would typically spend one day at base camp with each crew, making sure they were ready for the rigors of the trail. After that, he would escort the outfit for one to three days, until he was satisfied that they would be able to complete the trip on their own. Once he was confident in their ability, he would turn back to base camp to do the same thing with the next group coming up.

As one might imagine, it was rigorous work. The ranger was almost always on the move, guiding groups out, then rushing back to manage the next. He often ended up spending a lot of time on the trail by himself, scrambling over rocks and through forests under the summer sun. But, being a fit and energetic outdoor enthusiast, James relished the work. And he never encountered any difficulties he couldn't handle tramping through the wilderness. That all changed the day his route took him over Urraca Mesa.

It was a hot July afternoon, and James was returning to base camp after escorting a group that was hiking into the southern part of the ranch; this one was going to be a hard walk back. Urraca Mesa loomed between him and his destination, and he knew from experience that he had a strenuous climb ahead.

Did the ranger recall the stories of Urraca Mesa as he clambered up the rocky trail? Was there any trepidation, even a trace of fear in the back of his mind? None whatsoever. James was a pragmatic young man schooled in the United States Naval Academy. What's more, he was a pragmatic young man with a job ahead of him, to get down off the mesa and back to base camp as quickly as possible.

So he didn't even break his stride as he hit the top of the mesa, keeping up his brisk pace through the trees. He had just come upon a clearing when he was seized by a feeling that there was something behind him, something moving fast. All of Ben James' assumptions about Urraca Mesa were about to change.

The shove was violent and strong, hitting him in the back with enough force to send him tumbling to the ground. Tucking before he fell, James rolled with the blow, coming out of it on his feet, ready to face his assailant. But there was nobody there. Breathing deeply and forcing himself into calmness, Ben James looked quickly about the clearing. Still nothing. All was still. It was just the trees and the brush under a brilliant blue sky.

When it occurred to James that nothing could have moved that fast—hitting him with such force and then vanishing completely in mere seconds—he instinctively began to rationalize. It was impossible, something pushing him. There was no way. He told himself that he must have lost his footing or tripped on a rock; the sensation of being shoved had just been a product of his imagination.

Brushing himself off and readjusting his backpack, he started out again. But he wasn't even out of the clearing when he was shoved again. Once more the force hit him square in the back, this time far harder than before. For the second time in two minutes, James found himself tumbling to the ground. This blow was so fierce that he was unable to get up right away, but lay there winded, all too aware that whatever had struck him could easily hit him again. And yet as James lay there, defenseless and desperately trying to catch his breath, whatever had struck him did not press the attack.

By the time James regained his feet for the second time, there was no denying it. He was afraid. The attacks had come so quickly, without sound or warning, and James was painfully aware of how defenseless he was. Standing there in the middle of the clearing, afraid to move and equally afraid to stay, his eyes darted around, trying to survey everything in all directions at once. He only stood there for a few more seconds before his shaking legs carried him away, running across the clearing and once more into the woods. He would make it away from the mesa and down to the base camp without any more attacks that day. And yet this experience wouldn't be his only one on Urraca Mesa that summer.

James may have been curious about what exactly had happened on top of the mesa that day. Still, whatever curiosity possessed him was overshadowed by apprehension, and, keeping quiet about the affair, the ranger made it his practice to stay as far away from the mesa as he could. He was able to avoid the cursed promontory for the next two weeks, but necessity forced him back. This time, he was expected to go over the mesa in the dead of night.

A sprained ankle was the cause of it all. Not James' ankle, but one of the adult advisers who had been leading one of the hiking parties. James had been told to take this man's place, accompanying the hikers until their injured leader recovered. Several days later, James' crew got word that the leader's ankle had healed and he was on his way back. James was ordered back to base camp as fast as possible, because there was another group of hikers waiting for their orientation. He was expected to depart immediately.

James instantly recognized what the order meant. The sun was just beginning to set, and the most direct path to base camp was over Urraca Mesa. Obeying the order meant a trek across the mesa that night. He didn't really need to think about it. He still wasn't about to say anything about what had previously happened, and he wasn't about to set back a group of hikers because of it either. Steeling up his courage, he set out for the mesa, trying to keep his mind from thoughts of nameless evil lurking in the darkness.

Approaching the mesa from the south, he made the assent as quickly as he could, trying to ignore the fear pounding in his veins. Try as he might to shut out the memory of his last time on the mesa, there was no keeping down his mounting dread. Upon reaching Urraca's plateau, James' unease only got worse. He could not help but notice the silence over the mesa, huge and absolute. There wasn't a sound from any

No camping was allowed atop the mesa.

nocturnal birds, no coyotes howling, no insects chirping. Neither was there a breeze, and the grass and trees were so still that James might have been walking through a photograph.

He knew it in his bones. Whatever had accosted him before was there, somewhere on the mesa. Suddenly conscious of the beam of light from his flashlight, James turned it off, hoping to make it across the mesa as quickly and inconspicuously as possible, without attracting the attention of the thing that was up there. He strode down the path, moving as fast as he could in the limited light.

He had been walking like this for only a few minutes when he saw it—a small light flickering in the darkness about 40 yards from the trail. Stopping the instant he caught sight of it, James stood there for what seemed like a long time, holding his breath, trying to make sense of what he was seeing. It was a campfire. He could make out the flames now, licking at the darkness. There was also a figure next to the fire, barely visible in the circle of light.

Thoughts collided. No camping was allowed atop the mesa; as a ranger, it was his duty to enforce such regulations. But then there was also the fear, a cold sensation creeping up his back. Who would be up here at this hour, sitting by himself in front of a campfire? He looked at the lone figure again, and shuddered involuntarily.

Yet as spooked as he was by this lone figure sitting there in front of a fire on the plateau he had come to dread, James knew that he could not turn around and let this situation continue. He was a ranger, after all, and this was an illegal fire. Duty dictated that he would have to confront this individual.

James stepped off the trail and approached—slowly, cautiously. He was able to make out the scene as he drew closer. It was a Boy Scout sitting in front of his little fire and crying quietly. Nearing the ring of firelight, James was able to make out that the boy was no older than 15 and that he was dressed in a vintage scout uniform dating back to the 1940s. Everything about the situation was strange. Why was this boy here? What was it with his uniform?

James stepped into the ring of light and spoke in his gentlest voice, asking the boy if he was okay, if he needed any help. The scout didn't respond, and James took off his pack, sitting down slowly across from him. That was when the boy looked up, staring past James with terrified eyes. The boy's face was dangerously pale, with streaks of dirt across his cheeks. There was an ugly cut across his chin.

James uncertainty was instantly replaced by concern. "Are you lost?" he asked. "Did you get lost from your crew?"

The scout nodded. It was a barely perceptible motion, but at least James knew that, whatever had happened, the boy wasn't so rattled that he was beyond comprehension. He had heard the ranger; he was able to respond. Having no idea what this strange youngster's story was, James assumed he'd had some sort of accident and was in mild shock. "All right," he said, standing up. "I'm on my way to base camp. Grab your gear and I'll lead you there."

James didn't wait for a response, but turned and stooped to grab his pack off the ground. He heard two soft words from the fire behind him: "I can't." And then the lights went out. The ranger spun around in the sudden darkness, fighting rising currents of terror and confusion. He was alone in pitch black darkness. There was no fire, no teary-eyed boy scout. A quick survey of his surroundings revealed no trace of any campfire. That was it. James decided then and there it was time to get off the mesa, and he did so in a headlong rush. Throwing caution to the wind, he dug for his flashlight, switched it on, and ran all the way down to the base camp.

He wasn't so tight-lipped the second time around. Telling everyone he encountered as soon as he reached base camp, James soon learned that he had just had a run-in with one of the mesa's more frequently spotted spirits. According to his associates, the boy he had just seen was the famous "Lost Scout," the apparition of a youngster who had vanished on

He came face-to-face with the young Boy Scout.

the mesa many years ago. Though the boy's body was never found, he began appearing to startled trekkers soon after—sometimes alone, in front of a fire, looking frightened and hurt, and other times, just materializing on a trail and then vanishing without warning.

Michael Connelly cites the experience of Ray Warren, a serious-minded scout leader who also came face-to-face with the young apparition. Warren's encounter occurred in the broad daylight of early morning while he was guiding an expedition across the mesa. It happened shortly after they reached the top, while descending to Urraca Camp on the northern base. Rounding a curve in the trail, they came upon the boy in the old uniform, looking scared and lost.

Warren immediately began questioning the scout. Who was he? How did he get there? What crew was he with? But the boy was obviously in a state of shock and offered little in return, only muttering to the crowd of scouts that surrounded him that he was lost. Noting the scout's pallor, Warren offered him something to eat and drink, but the youngster just shook his head silently.

Warren and his crew were trying to take the boy's appearance in stride, but it was all they could do not to stand and gape. Though he seemed real, solid enough to reach out and touch, it was clear that something about this boy was very wrong. Not only was he dressed in an antiquated uniform, but there was a *feeling* about him. Connelly describes it as a "weird dream" that the boys had stepped into. Nevertheless, no one intended to leave this strange scout on his own, and Warren told him to join his squad.

The boy did as he was told, falling in with his fellow scouts, head down and quiet. When Warren ordered a rest at the edge of the mesa, the mysterious joiner once again refused offers of food and water. Warren began to worry then, thinking that the boy was in shock, and in need of medical attention. To this end, Warren called for the scouts to move out, endeavoring to make it down to the base camp as quickly as possible.

They hadn't gone farther than a few yards when a frightened shout sounded from the back of the line, followed by several scouts calling to their leader. "Mr. Warren!" one of the scouts called out. "The kid's gone! He was walking right in front of me and he just disappeared."

Another scout who was standing right there was just as stupefied, saying that the boy had just vanished into thin air, right where he stood, when they reached the edge of the mesa. Warren looked at the boys; even if they had been making this up, the group was standing in the middle of open ground. If he was hiding, there was no way he would have been able to vanish from sight so quickly. Nevertheless, Warren ordered a search, and the march was temporarily halted as the group fanned to look for the weird boy. They found no trace of his passing.

By the time they set out again for base camp, Warren and his crew knew that they had been in the presence of something unnatural. Warren had no desire to scare the boys any more than they had been, so he didn't say anything when, turning around to take a final look as they were descending, he saw the lost scout standing there. The boy was transparent now, the sky clearly visible right through him. He was at the edge of the mesa, a hand raised in farewell, tears streaming down his grief-stricken face. Warren looked on in silence as the figure became more and more transparent, until he vanished from sight altogether.

When they arrived at base camp, Warren and his troop wasted no time reporting their encounter. They were told the same thing as Ben James, and so many others before. They had just had a run with the famous Lost Scout, the soul of the tragic youngster who mysteriously vanished so many years ago.

The Good Spirit of Begashibito Canyon

The Navajo of northern Arizona call him "the Good Spirit," and he has been around for as long as anyone can remember. He often appears as a smiling old man, wandering alone among sun-baked arroyos, dressed in rough gray robes with a rope tied around the waist, or else wrapped in a splendid Navajo blanket, with grass sandals on his feet and a leather band around his head. Yet while his wardrobe has been known to change, he comes only when he is desperately needed, with a peaceful smile and lifesaving succor.

Hosteen Black Goat was a man who desperately needed the Good Spirit. He was lost. Somehow, his journey had led him to Begashibito Canyon in the midst of a sandstorm. The storm had become so bad that he could see no more than a few feet in front of him. Not that it mattered; he was no longer going anywhere. The intensity of the storm had just picked up, and the horse he was riding was no longer manageable, bucking and rearing in the roaring wind and cutting sand. Hosteen Black Goat clung to the animal's mane as a drowning man would a life preserver, knowing full well that he would not be able to stay on for much longer.

Then something incredible happened. He knew it instantly; the sand stopped stabbing at his face and the exposed skin on his arms and legs. His horse stopped its violent bucking and rearing. He dared to open one eye, then the other, to find that even though the storm continued to rage around him, he and his horse were sheltered from it as though they were in an invisible tunnel that stretched out

The Good Spirit has been the guardian for many travelers through desert storms.

before them. They were still in the heart of the sandstorm, but somehow were being spared the worst of it.

That was when Black Goat saw him—through the sand, a dim outline of a man. And there was the call, a faint sound over the howling wind, beckoning for him to follow. Hosteen Black Goat nudged his horse, finding to his surprise that the animal responded. Horse and master crept forward, always several yards behind the man who was leading them, continuing until they were safely through the canyon. That was when the man got his first and only clear look at the man who had led him out. He was old, with a gray beard, kind eyes and a Navajo blanket around his shoulders. The old man looked at the rider for just a few seconds before vanishing from sight.

Another well-known account of the Good Spirit involves another rider facing more extreme weather—this time a woman, stranded against the steep edge of an arroyo during a violent summer storm. The rain started suddenly, a torrential downpour that began with a flash of lightning and a clap of thunder while she was navigating the canyon. The last thing she saw before sheets of rain obstructed her vision was the lip of an arroyo and the sheer drop beyond. She knew her place on the ledge was precarious, but she dared not direct her horse as she could barely see an inch beyond the beast's ears. The horse began to creep forward on its own, and when the woman pulled back on its mane in an effort to stop it, she felt the animal tense. The storm and her own uncertainty had pushed the horse near panic, and she felt disaster looming—in the form of the edge of a precipice just beyond her vision.

The moment she felt the cold shock of panic coming over her, she heard a gentle voice and was instantly calmed. It was not the words that calmed her; indeed, she couldn't make out the words over the cacophony of the storm. It was the tone of his voice—strong and gentle—that did it. She knew that her horse had heard it too, because she felt the animal relax underneath her. Another bolt of lightening streaked through the sky, followed by an earsplitting thunderclap, and for an instant she was sure that her horse would bolt. But it did not. It stayed still and calm, its ears perked for the sound of the man's voice, which could still be heard through the storm.

Then she saw him, the old man wrapped in the Navajo blanket, gesturing for her to come forward. This woman knew all about the legend of the Good Spirit of Begashibito Canyon, and realized with a rush of joy that this was who she was looking at. The Good Spirit had come to help her navigate her way through the storm. And, as it turned out, deliver her from certain death. For not one minute after the old man had guided her away from the arroyo's edge, she heard a mighty roar, and turned just in time to see a flash flood engulf the place where she and her horse had just been. Knowing that she was safe now, she turned and thanked the Good Spirit for leading her and her horse away from disaster. The old man returned her smile and vanished into the rain.

There is also the story of the three young children who wandered away from their mother and got lost in the desert. It was shearing season, and their mother was working in a sheep camp when the trio got the notion of adventure in their heads and wandered off to find it. By nightfall, the mother, frantic with worry, had alerted the whole camp, and everyone began searching for any sign of the youngsters.

The old man vanished within seconds.

They were found several miles away the next morning, completely calm and heading back toward camp, certain that they were going in the right direction. The search party thought it odd that such young children would be so sure of their ability to find their way back home. When the youngsters were asked how they knew they were going the right way, the eldest replied: "There was an old man who wore a long gray coat. He told us he knew the way back to camp, and told us to follow him."

"Where is this old man now?" someone asked.

"He is gone," the eldest boy spoke up again. "He disappeared when he saw you coming."

No one from the search party questioned the trio about this man, how he knew the way back to the camp, or how it was possible that he just vanished into thin air. They didn't ask because they knew—it was the Good Spirit of Begashibito Canyon.

Another more recent account is narrated by Jane Eppinga in her book, *Arizona Twilight Tales: Good Ghosts, Evil Spirits & Blue Ladies*. This incident has a man named Bill Carlen encountering the Good Spirit while going about his work along the Begashibito Canyon. As far as jobs go, Carlen's occupation repairing windmills was hardly typical. Nor was it easy. Every now and then his work required him to do maintainance on far-flung windmills in isolated parts of the canyon.

On one such excursion, an exhausted Carlen found himself driving his pickup truck over one of the more treacherous stretches of road in the region. Winding along the edge of the canyon, the road was narrow and strewn with rocks—certainly white knuckle driving for most motorists. But the route had become quite routine for Bill Carlen, and, being a little bit short on sleep that day, he actually found the bumps and jolts on the road comforting, relaxing even. His truck was a cradle and he was being rocked to sleep, his eyes growing heavier with every mile.

He was almost asleep, his head just starting to sink into his lap, when he registered a sight on the road that jolted him awake. It was a man standing on the road, mere yards in front of his truck. He slammed on the brakes, but it was too late; his truck skidded over the elderly man. Carlen jumped out, his stomach in his throat, his legs shaking in terror. He was convinced that he had just run over the man. But there was no mark on his grill. Falling to his hands and knees he looked underneath his truck, but there was no one there. It occurred to him, then, that there had been no jolt of impact when he hit the man.

He began running over the details of the incident in his mind. Finally, he noticed that he had stopped his truck so close to the lip of the canyon that the grill was actually hanging over it. Carlen's blood ran cold when the realization struck him: if the old man hadn't surprised him awake and made him slam on the brakes, he would have driven right over the edge.

Thus the Good Spirit is credited for having saved another Begashibito Canyon traveler from certain death. But who, exactly, is the Good Spirit? And why, of all places, has he chosen to patrol this one canyon in northern Arizona? While no explanation can be completely trusted, the most common theory is that this elderly man is the spirit of one of the first Franciscan monks in the area. Some have even gone so far as to attach a name: Fray Hernando de Escalante, a holy man and explorer who, in the late 18th century, was one of the earliest Europeans to walk through the Hopi villages in the area, attempting to convert the natives to Christianity. It is also said that he may have been among the first Europeans to cross the Colorado River.

According to local legend, when de Escalante passed through, he found corn near the village of Oraibi. In a very public ceremony, he blessed the corn, offering a prayer of thanks and asking that good spirits prevent harm from befalling the people in the area. Could de Escalante have known while he was praying that *he* would become the canyon's protector after he passed? An eternity of watching over foolhardy wanderers making their way across a secluded canyon—some might call this nothing less than a condemnation. But for whatever reason, the Good Spirit maintains his vigil, and, if sightings of this smiling apparition are to be believed, does so happily.

The Rock That Burns Atop Music Mountain

No one knew where he came from, the man with the shining blond hair and the burning blue eyes. He had a fine and youthful face, but a body that was old and shriveled. None among the Hualapais who lived in those mountains knew where he came from, nor who he was, but there was no doubt that he was a man of great medicine. His healing powers came from his eyes. It was said that sometimes, all he needed to do was fix his burning eyes on the sick, and they would be healed—that just the light from his eyes could cure the most serious illness.

The whole band was amazed at this man's powers. Not only was he able to heal with a glance, but he held sway over the creatures of the land. With a mere gesture the most wild and fearsome animals and insects that dwelt among the rocks would become kind and gentle. He was seen with rattlesnakes draped around his neck, petting vultures and communing with scorpions. His powers were such that the Hualapai chief quickly made the stranger a medicine man, and for many years, the band enjoyed the best health and good fortune.

But trouble was to come with the chief's favorite son, who grew to be a tall, powerful and respected warrior. It came to pass that this young man fell in love with the most beautiful woman in the village. He decided asked her to marry him, and she happily accepted. Grand preparations were made for the ceremony, and on the day of the wedding, everyone woke in great anticipation of the celebration that day. But it was not long after the sun peaked over the horizon that a terrible cry sounded from the home of the bride's family. She was gone, vanished on the day she was to be wed. They looked and they looked, but the jewel of the tribe was nowhere to be found. And while they searched through the village, they discovered something else—the medicine man with the shining blond hair and burning blue eyes was also gone.

Had the pair—two of the band's most valued members—been abducted by enemies? Was there an unknown evil at work? Had the powerful medicine man, still a mystery to them after so many years, abducted the beautiful young woman? Or had she willingly run off with the medicine man?

Later that day, an old toothless hag stumbled into the village with news that spared the warrior his esteem in the eyes of the villagers. The old woman barged onto the confused and sorrowful scene, shouting out that she had seen the young bride and the medicine man with the shriveled body with her own eyes. They were together, near the peak of one of the greatest mountains in the range.

The chief did not waste a moment's time. He ordered all his braves to go up to the mountain peak and reclaim his son's bride and the medicine man who had so sullied his son's honor. And so it was that the Hualapai men went up to the mountain peak and found the pair, just as the old woman had said. They were sitting together near a large, smooth rock when the warriors came upon them. Though they were brave and strong men, they all trembled before the fierce gaze of the medicine man. None of them dared to raise a hand against him, but they told him that the chief wanted to see him one last time, to know why he had done such a thing to dishonor the chief's son.

The medicine man agreed to go back with them. He was presented to the chief later that same day, yet deigned to say nothing, offering no explanation or excuse for his actions. So it was that the chief pronounced the medicine man's exile, ordering him to leave the village at first light. The village braves would follow him out to make sure that he left, but the chief made it clear that, while the medicine man was in their company, no harm was to come to him who had once done so much good for his people. Little did the chief know that such an order was a waste of breath—that indeed, it wasn't the medicine man who was in imminent danger, but those who were escorting him.

The braves that were sent out with the medicine man were the finest warriors in the village. They were bold and strong and had all confronted many dangers. None of them had any fear in their hearts for the medicine man. It was true that his eyes burned with a disturbing fire, and that none of them had ever seen hair the color of the sun, but the man's body was weak, so frail that he walked slowly and with some difficulty over the rocky peaks. Slowing their pace to that of the medicine man, the warriors grew impatient. They muttered their frustrations to each other, wondering why their chief had deemed it necessary to put this feeble man under the guard of men such as themselves. What threat would he ever pose to them or their village? It was absurd.

The medicine man heard the men grumbling, and after a while he spoke. "I agree there should not be so many of you. So many strong young warriors ordered to guard one sick and frail man, there is no sense in it. Your chief has not made a wise decision."

"Be quiet, fool," the leader of the escort barked. "Our chief is a great man who has led our people through many trials. If he says we are to accompany you away from these lands, then that is what we shall do." The man had spoken fiercely, but it was clear by the look in his eyes that a fear was growing inside of him. His warrior's instinct was telling him that something was wrong, that he and his fellow braves were in danger. He did not know what this danger was—there were no enemies nearby, and they were in no danger of being overcome by the medicine man. But he felt it in his bones—a threat he did not understand, but a threat nonetheless.

More and more of the braves fell under the thrall of this growing foreboding as they walked on. It was a threat they did not understand. Yet the unease in their stomachs, the electricity running up and down their spines and the nervousness coursing through their veins were their bodies' way of telling them that they were about to go into battle, though there was no enemy in sight.

When the realization came, it came to all of them at once. They were not guiding the medicine man out of the mountains, *he* was leading *them*. One by one the braves tried to stop their legs, to quit the march, only to find that they couldn't. They were not in control of themselves. Their steps had been taken over by some intangible and irresistible force, matching the blond-haired man's ponderous pace up the mountain. The medicine man had taken control.

They continued their march up the side of the mountain, like so many sheep after their shepherd, until they came up near the top of a rocky peak just as the sun was beginning to set. There was something in the blood red sky that sent tremors of terror through the gathered braves. But they did not cry out because they could not cry out. They had become like statues in the day's last light, only able to stand and stare in horror as the medicine man raised his voice to the scarlet sky above and called upon the gods. The blue light in the medicine man's eyes became painful to look at. And then they noticed it for the first time—the large rock next to the medicine man had begun to glow. Although only a faint blue at first, it became brighter and brighter by the second, growing more powerful as the medicine man chanted until it could be seen for miles around, a burning blue light atop the mountain.

That was when they began to die. One by one, the braves fell where they stood. They died on their feet, stricken down by something lethal and unseen in the light. The medicine man continued to chant, not stopping until the last warrior fell dead—the same expression of terror and surprise on his face as on all the others. Only then did the medicine man cease, and the light in his eyes dimmed, as did the light in the burning rock beside him. Alone, he gazed for a moment at the range of peaks that stabbed at the first stars in the violet sky, then continued on, slowly trudging into exile.

The braves were discovered days later, their bloated bodies clustered around the rock, and no sign at all of the medicine man. He was gone. No one would ever see the powerful stranger again, though he cost them the lives of every one of their best warriors.

From that day on, the mountaintop was considered a cursed place. And the rock the braves died around, a relic of evil, believed by the Hualapais to contain the energy of an evil god. They avoided the peak for many years.

It wasn't until 1854, when Lieutenant Joseph C. Ives discovered the mountain for the United States, that the legend of the Hualapais' evil rock spread beyond the region. Thinking that the strata on the side of the mountain resembled sheet music, Ives named the peak Music Mountain. The site of the blue rock, however, is not so pleasantly named.

Squatting on the lip of a chasm called Death Trap Gorge, amid a sprawling cluster of bleached bones, the rock is said to glow with a faint blue light and be lethal to anyone who touches it. The following account is given of a group of hunters exploring the area with a Hualapai guide in 1895.

Approaching the edge of the gorge, the group caught sight of a bighorn sheep near the rock. One moment wondering at the dim glow coming off the rock, the next moment the hunters were staring agape as it flared up bright blue the instant the sheep touched it. Less than a second later, the burning light faded to a dim glow, and the now-lifeless sheep went tottering into the gorge.

The stupefied silence was broken by one of the hunters. "Did you see that?" came the urgent hiss. There was no answer, but the hunters crept forward as one, eager to get a closer look at the glowing blue rock.

That was when their Hualapai guide stepped forward. "Do not take another step," he said, "lest the god in the stone kill you too." He gestured to the ground around the gorge, and for the first time the hunters noticed the countless bones scattered across the ground. "This rock holds an ancient evil," their guide continued, "and no living thing has ever touched it and lived."

So it was that the rock on Music Mountain in northern Arizona was left undisturbed, and little has been said of it since then. Perhaps the local Hualapais have been successful in steering curiosity-seekers away. Or perhaps the god in the rock has moved on, and the rock has lost its cold glow. Whatever the case, hikers in the old Hualapais territory might do well to exercise caution and steer away from any glowing, blue boulders. In this part of the world, the folklore tells us that an ancient evil may reside within. And no one needs to be told that ancient evil is best left alone.

The Curse of the Long Salt Clan

They are called the *Chindi*, dark spirits born of the parched earth of northern Arizona, terrorizing the denizens of the desiccated landscape for one sole purpose—vengeance. Navajo mythology tells us that the *Chindi* naturally reside in a formless spirit world, coming to the earth only if they are summoned, to tirelessly pursue absolute and complete revenge.

Revenge for what? For whatever wrongs have been called to their attention. The *Chindi* are drawn by powerful magic, by the songs of those who have suffered some injustice at the hands of another and need to see it rectified. And yet according to Navajo legend, the *Chindi* do not measure justice by human standards; the punishments they exact on their victims are usually grossly out of proportion with the offense. The folklore suggests a massive divide between the notion of revenge and fair punishment. Indeed, there is nothing just about the retribution that these vengeance spirits seek, and *Chindi*, along with those medicine men who are able to summon them, are among the most feared by the Navajo. The legend of the Long Salt clan is, if nothing else, a cautionary tale about what happens to those who think themselves above the medicine man and the powers he is able to summon.

The tale begins in the early 1800s with a feud between two Navajo clans. The feud ultimately led to the murder of a man named Dawn Dancer at the hands of the Long Salt family. Yet the spirit of Dawn Dancer did not go quietly to his grave. He began tormenting the Long Salts, haunting their sleep and their waking hours until finally settling on the man who had murdered him. The murderer was tormented to the brink of madness. Not enjoying even a moment of peace, everywhere this man looked he saw visions of his victim, blood splattered and pale as death, uttering a voiceless curse at the Long Salt who took his life.

So it was that the Long Salts sought out the aid of a medicine man. They went to a solitary shaman who, though blind and bent with age, was reputed to be one of the most powerful medicine men in the area. The old man listened to the Long Salts' problem, then promised that it would take some work, but he would convince the bitter spirit to leave the family in peace. It took him three days and three nights. Three days and three nights of singing over the body of the man who had killed Dawn Dancer. Three days and three nights of communion with the angry spirit, until, at last, the murderer felt the hateful presence of the spirit that had plagued him vanish. He was cured. The medicine man's magic had worked.

The murderer cured, the time had come for the Long Salts to pay for the medicine man's services. Appearing before the family elders, the old medicine man requested that he be given four of the best sheep from the Long Salt's flock, and two men from the family were sent out to fulfill the request—two men whose names would be cursed by several generations to follow.

The pair went out looking for the sheep, but it wasn't long before they grew tired of their task. Their family hogan was a great distance from where the flock was gathered, and separating out the best of their flock seemed like a lot of work.

And ludicrous, also, as they told themselves that there was no way the medicine man, blind and old as he was, would be able to know if he was getting the best sheep. Indeed, once the animals were slaughtered and presented, how would he know if they were even sheep? It was laziness that finally decided them. Not about to spend hours scouring the flock for their finest animals, the two men opted to kill a number of nearby antelope instead. They would present the carcasses of these animals as payment, thinking that the medicine man would be none the wiser.

They certainly fooled the elders from their own clan, who took the carcasses to the medicine man without asking any questions. The medicine man accepted the four butchered animals without a word, and for a few weeks, at least, it looked as though the business was concluded. Then the first Long Salt fell ill.

It was a sickness that none of them had seen before. One day, he had been perfectly healthy; the next, he was too weak to rise from bed and could not stomach food or water. In a period of two days, right before his family's eyes, the man wasted away and died. The Long Salts' mourning turned to fear when another of their number awoke stricken with the same weakness and pallor just a few days after this man passed. Within the week, this man was dead as well. But even before he was gone, another of the Long Salts was bedridden with the mysterious illness.

The lethal epidemic spread through the bewildered Long Salt family. The wise men in the family began to suspect that someone had summoned a *Chindi* to wreak havoc on them, but none of them were sure why. Certainly none of the Long Salts' known enemies were powerful enough to harness such magic. No one had any idea who had cast this curse upon them—no one, that is, save the two men who had presented four antelope carcasses in place of sheep. The deed was foremost in their minds as, one by one, members of their family succumbed to sickness. It was a terrible secret they carried, and their horror mounted with each death. Would they ultimately be responsible for the extinction of their clan?

Finally unable to bear the secret any longer, they confessed their deed to the Long Salt elders, who promptly went back to the medicine man with these men in tow, desperate to make amends for the great wrong. With tearful contrition, the two men told the medicine man what they had told their elders. They did not mean to cheat the medicine man out of any sort of maliciousness; they were guilty of indolence, nothing more, and were ready to offer anything to save their family from the curse that had been set upon them.

The medicine man then confirmed their worst fears. Upon discovering the Long Salts' trickery, he had indeed set a *Chindi* upon them. It was the vengeance demon that was killing them with disease, and it would likely not stop until each and every one of them was dead. The two men, along with the Long Salt elders, pleaded with the medicine man to call off the terrible demon.

The medicine man was quiet for a long moment. The only thing that was more strenuous than summoning a *Chindi* was mustering the magic to call one back. And to do such a thing for two men who dared deceive a man as powerful as he? He would have to think about it. "Come back in 10 days' time," he finally said to the men assembled before him, "and I will give you my answer."

Ten days is a long time when one's family members are dying daily. But the Long Salts did not dare raise any objection with the old man. They went away for 10 days while the *Chindi* continued to exact its brutal vengeance. They waited as their brothers and sisters, parents and children died before their eyes. They told themselves that they only had to wait 10 days, and that there was no way the angry old medicine man would allow the *Chindi* to continue simply because of two men's laziness. But they would never know whether or not this was actually the case.

For, to their horror, when they returned 10 days later, they discovered that the one man who had the power to call off the *Chindi* had succumbed to old age. The medicine man was dead, and the Long Salts were alone to face an entity they could not stop—an entity bent on their destruction.

The *Chindi* took its time, and generations of Long Salts felt its wrath. The first of them had died in the early 1800s, but there were enough of them being born throughout the 19th century to keep the vengeance demon occupied. It did its work slowly, so that the number of Long Salts was whittled down gradually over the course of 100 years.

By 1925 there were only three of them left. And then within that year, two of the three became sick and died. The last of the clan was a young girl named Alice Long Salt. She was under the care of a Navajo man who was appalled at the fate of the Long Salt family. Unable to come to terms with the fact that hundreds of people had been killed by a single act of nonchalant laziness nearly a century ago, he took it on himself to keep Alice Long Salt alive.

He did everything in his power. He went to other medicine men hoping that they would be able to call off the

Chindi, but found no one able to do it. Thinking that she may be able to physically stay ahead of the *Chindi* if he kept her moving, the man relocated the young girl frequently, moving her from house to house and village to village.

It seemed to work for a while. For three years, Alice kept the Long Salt name alive, though she was living a life of constant displacement while a demon she could not see wanted her dead for a reason she could not comprehend. Some say that benevolent forces came to their aid during this time. That, for instance, a good spirit in the form of an owl had taken to warning them when the *Chindi* was approaching. Whenever Alice's protector was woken in the middle of the night by loud hoots coming from the darkness nearby, he learned to wake his charge, pack up and go at that moment.

It is impossible to say whether such extraordinary measures kept Alice alive, or whether it was merely a desire on the *Chindi's* part to prolong the agony for as long as possible. Alice lived on for three years, the longest amount of time that had gone by without a Long Salt perishing since the early 1800s. Yet like all the others, when death came, it came suddenly.

She was in good health on the cold winter day she and her guardian stumbled on an abandoned hogan near Red Mesa. There was a snowstorm raging, and her face was flushed with cold while she helped build a fire. If they would be safe anywhere, the man who was watching over her thought, it would be here, in this secluded hogan, in the middle of a snowstorm.

Yet it was then and there that the *Chindi* who had plagued the Long Salts for so many years dealt its final blow. Sometime in her sleep Alice became ill, and by the time she woke, she was not able to rise from her sleeping roll. She died two days later, still lying in the hogan as the winter wind whistled through the cracks in the decrepit shelter. And the man looking over her wept at the passing of the last Long Salt—a little girl whose life was snuffed out by a remorseless demon, which, only now, after more than 100 years, was content with the vengeance it had exacted.

4
Modern Hauntings and Urban Legends

A Helpful Haunt in Phoenix

Imaginary friends are common enough for children, but adults claiming to enjoy the presence of invisible companions are usually cause for concern. "When I think about it now, that was probably what was scaring me most," says our eyewitness, who shall go by the pseudonym Anthony Taylor. "I was really wondering if I was losing my mind, and that was what was really hard to swallow. Sudden cold spots in a room, your cup of coffee making itself—I knew I could cope with all the weird stuff that was going on, just as long as I knew for sure that it was actually happening."

Anthony and his wife made the move to Phoenix in the late '90s. "My wife's a nurse, and she got a great job offer in one of the hospitals. We took it, and it was great for her, but for those first few months I was in limbo." A self-described introvert without any work lined up when he arrived, Anthony spent a lot of time alone. "It wasn't just a matter of finding work," he says. "I wasn't really sure what I wanted to do. I still didn't have a career lined up or anything, and was thinking that I might go back to school, but I didn't really know what I wanted to study."

With his wife often working for the better part of the day, Anthony found himself turning inward, mulling over the direction of his life. "We were in a new place, and I didn't really know anyone," he says. "It was new to me, spending that much time alone, and it just made things that much weirder when the house..." he pauses, "...came to life."

One thing often said of houses purported to be haunted is that there's a definite *feel* within them—whether it is an inexplicable foreboding, a physical chill or an undeniable sense that there's *something* present. Anthony claims that this certainly wasn't the case in his Phoenix home. "There was nothing unusual about this place," he says. "It was an almost brand new bungalow in the suburbs. An old couple lived in it before us, and moved out to be closer to their grandchildren. As far as I know, no one died here. It had big windows, clean carpet and a bright kitchen," Anthony laughs. "Real *House and Home Magazine* place." In other words, nothing at all like the three-story Victorian Amityville-type homes that people tend to associate with ghosts. That isn't to say that Anthony settled in easily.

"I was spending way too much time indoors those first few months," he says, "and if there was anything strange going on, I wouldn't be surprised if I was missing most of it." Missing most, but not all. For it wasn't long before Anthony had his first bizarre experience in the Phoenix bungalow. "My routine was to get up at around 10-ish and put coffee on first thing," Anthony begins. "A lot of the time, though, I'd get caught up with a magazine or a TV show and forget that I'd put hot water on. Sometimes I'd end up reboiling that water two or three times before I'd have my cup of coffee. Like I said, I was pretty out of it then."

So, he felt he had reason to doubt himself when he walked into the kitchen late one morning and came face-to-face with the inexplicable. "One thing I knew for sure is that I'd turned the kettle on twice that morning," he says. "I'd forgotten about the water once, and turned it on to boil again. When I went back about 10 minutes later, there was a full cup of coffee on the kitchen counter, with cream."

Dumbstruck, Anthony's first assumption was that he had actually made himself the coffee and forgotten about it. "I'm telling you, it was a real '*Uh-oh, I'm nuts*' moment. I didn't even think about the possibility of a ghost or anything in the house at that point. My thinking was that it was just a matter of me being way too much in my head." Not that it made the experience any less frightening. Taking it as a signal that he was spending too much time alone with his thoughts, he began making an effort to venture out of his house *and* his head from time to time. Yet the more he concentrated on his surroundings, the more he came to realize that all sorts of weird things were going on.

"I really started to worry about my noggin at that point," Anthony continues. "I'd never really seriously thought about whether or not ghosts were real. I think the problem was that none of the things that were going on were too overtly weird. It wasn't like anything out of *Poltergeist*, with furniture flying around or dead people coming out of the walls...where you can say: 'All right, now there's definitely something going on here.' "

Anthony's accounts reveal a spirit that had an apparent fascination for detail, manifesting itself through minute, almost unnoticeable behavior. "It's funny, looking back I always feel like it was shy at first. That's why it started so small." So small, that the occurrences would only by noticed by someone paying close attention. "They were always inconsequential but helpful little things," Anthony says, "like the toothpaste. My wife and I had never capped the toothpaste. Some people might think it's gross, but I'd gotten used to scraping away a crust of toothpaste every time I brushed my teeth. It was like that for as long as we'd been married. Anyway, one day that changed. The tube was always capped and put away." Anthony didn't think too much of it, assuming that his wife was making an effort to get tidier, until the day she mentioned it at the dinner table. "We were having supper and she brought it up out of the blue. She said something like, one good thing about me staying at home was that there was somebody keeping the place tidier. I asked her what she meant, she brought up the toothpaste—said it was about time we got in the habit. I didn't correct her." Anthony laughs. "I took the credit. I wasn't working, and could use all the help I could I get."

While he's able to laugh now, Anthony goes on to say that at the time, he really doubted himself. "Like I said, ghosts really weren't on my mind at that point. I just remember thinking that, hell, maybe I *did* start capping the toothpaste. Maybe I could've and forgot it. God knows I was forgetting all sorts of things."

It wasn't just the toothpaste. There was also the issue of the keys. "I started getting wise to the keys about a week after my wife started work. No matter where I threw them when I got in, when it was time to go they were always back where they should be—on the key hooks by the door." Anthony goes on to explain that this was strange because he had never used the key hooks. "That was one of my wife's ideas. She put it up because I was always losing my keys. But I don't think I ever remember using it. Not once." The first few times it happened, Anthony tore the place apart looking for his keys, only to find them hanging where they ought to be. "After that, the key rack was the first place I looked, and every time, that's always where they were."

That was when Anthony really began to wonder about what was going on. "I really started taking notice after the situation with the keys," he says. "That one wasn't easy to ignore. I didn't lose my keys *every* time I left the house. There were times when I *knew* that I'd put the keys on the coffee table. But when I'd head out again, there they were on the key rack." Still unwilling to consider the possibility of the supernatural, Anthony just became more diligent about where he put his key chain. "The experience definitely made me more conscious of things I didn't really think about before," he says. Rather than deal with whatever was going on in his house, Anthony took to making certain he put his keys on the hook after he stepped in. "This way I knew for sure they weren't going anywhere," he says. "I didn't like the idea that there was something in the house rearranging my things any better than the thought that I might be losing my mind."

Just as Anthony began suspecting causes besides incredible absentmindedness, one event occurred that convinced him there were mysterious forces at work in his new home. "It was the only time I actually got scared," he says. "It was such a little thing, but it happened so fast that it shocked the hell out of me." Sitting on the living room sofa eating his breakfast and watching the morning news, Anthony stubbed his toe when he got up to put his plate back in the kitchen. Stumbling in pain he fell against the wall, knocking a framed photograph askew. He continued to the kitchen, limping the whole way. "I put the plate in the sink, paced a few times to walk off the pain. It couldn't have been more than a minute—tops. When I walked back to the living room, one look and I felt chills go up my back." The photograph that he'd left hanging lopsided had been perfectly straightened.

Shaken as he was, Anthony explains that things got better for him after that morning. "I felt a lot clearer after that," he says. "I think a lot of people would think that you'd be scared stiff, but I was just glad that I wasn't going crazy. At that point, I knew something was up. There was no doubt in my mind. It was a ghost. I was like, okay, so our bungalow's haunted."

Anthony got used to his invisible housemate soon after that, resigning himself to the fact that he had a supernatural companion. "Whoever or whatever it is, at least it's helpful," he says. "Personally, if I thought about ghosts before, it probably would've been in that *Shining, Poltergeist* horror movie kind of way. A mean ugly thing that scares the hell out of you, takes over your mind or, you know, drives you out of your house. Well, not the ghost we've got living with us.

"I eventually ended up getting a job," he says, "but by then, I really got used to the company." Laughing, Anthony goes on to say that not only did he appreciate the fact that there was someone else in the house with him, but that this someone else was so helpful. "The spirit got more active as the days passed. By the time I started up nine to five, all I had to do was put my water in the kettle, and about half the time, I'd come back to a full cup of Joe. It was brilliant." Anthony claims that the only thing he found unsettling about the haunt was its tendency to make the temperature in a room plummet.

"That was something that was happening more and more," he says. "I still think that its presence was getting stronger the longer we stayed. Who knows? Maybe it was getting comfortable with us being there, but that living room would get ice-cold some of those mornings. It came around when I was having breakfast in front of the TV. Sometimes it'd get so cold that I'd have to go outside and take a walk. The temperature would always be back to normal by the time I got back."

With the exception of the cold spells, Anthony got along fine with the spirit in the house. "I know this will sound strange to someone who's never met my wife, but I never told her what was going on in the house. I knew she was really busy with her new job and all, but more than that, she's just not the kind of person who'd be able to deal with that kind of information—she's a real worrier. First she'd worry about me. My thinking was the less drama, the better."

Now that Anthony was out of the house working, he noticed the goings-on in the house less and less. He and his wife ended up moving into another house two years later; by then, if the mysterious force was still present, its manifestations were so minor that they were escaping Anthony's notice entirely. "I don't know what to say. In the two years I lived there, I didn't really think about looking into what was going on, or why. I guess I assumed it was a ghost or something, but it could've just as easily been an alien or Buddha or the invisible man. The only concrete feeling I got was that *it*—whatever it was—was a bit on the shy side. That it *could've* been a lot more obvious. If it wanted to, it could've made all sorts of problems, but it wasn't sure what to make of us."

Whatever the case, Anthony ended up leaving the house without learning anything about the entity there. Besides a cursory look at the bungalow's history, which turned up nothing, Anthony wasn't interested in getting to the bottom of the phenomenon. The transition of the recent move was enough for him and his wife to deal with, and as long as it didn't disrupt his day-to-day life too much, he was content to leave it alone. Perhaps this approach is the same one the current residents have, assuming, that is, they've even noticed.

The Thing That Happened at Bonito Lake

"There's a real religious community that runs Bonito Park," begins our contact, "so I never really felt 100 percent comfortable talking about what happened." Assured that many sources only agree to talk about their supernatural experiences on condition of anonymity, the New Mexico resident agreed to tell his story. For the sake of this narrative, he shall be called "Jason Andrews."

Besides the occasional horror movie, Jason never gave much thought to the idea of ghosts. "I don't think I'd say that I did or didn't believe in them," he says. "Really, the whole subject didn't interest me too much. I'd never seen one before, and I didn't know anybody that did. So I didn't really think about it." That would change in the late '90s, during a camping trip to Bonito Park.

Located off Highway 37, near Ruidoso, New Mexico, Bonito Park is known for its natural beauty and is a place where people go to camp, fish and enjoy what the outdoors have to offer. More than a recreational spot, however, the park is also interesting among history enthusiasts. The site of a long-expired gold-mining operation, the park is said to contain many discarded relics from that time. They are mostly around Bonito Lake, where campers have found old lanterns and mining carts and ruined entrances into deserted mines. Close to one cluster of campsites stands an old ramshackle house, long abandoned by the gold-miner who set up there.

This was where our source, Jason Andrews, camped one summer weekend a few years ago. "I was out with my nephew and his best friend," Jason says. "Both of them were 11 years old—good kids, except maybe too much energy for their own good sometimes." Not that this was ever a problem for Jason. Claiming that he often felt as if he had more in common with his nephew than his 35-year-old brother, Jason looked forward to those weekends when his brother would ask him if he could take his son off his hands for a day or two.

"Nothing out of the ordinary happened that day," he says. "We did a bit of fishing, hiked around—had fun." They didn't catch any fish and ended up roasting hot dogs over the fire, exchanging the customary scary stories. "I really tried my hardest to scare those boys that night," Jason says. "But it was no good. They'd heard them all: the hook, the ax-murderer, the escaped convict from the nearby prison. I guess by 11 years old, these kids were scare-proof." The irony of what would occur later that night isn't lost on Jason. "Funny that I ended up being the one who got scared out of his wits."

It was about 10:30 and the fire had been reduced to embers when Jason told the boys it was time to call it a night. "As usual, that's when kids get their second wind, and I could hear them laughing and goofing off when they were getting into their tent." Calling over that they had best get to sleep, as they were going to have an early start the next day, Jason then switched on a flashlight to do some reading.

"I could hear them talking for a bit longer," he says, "but it got quiet pretty quick." Jason stresses that the book he was reading was nothing even remotely scary. "It was a history book," he says, "a biography on Alexander Hamilton, if you have to know. So whatever you want to say about what ended up happening, you can't say that it was inspired by my reading material." Although the ghost of Alexander Hamilton *has* been spotted by some people, the sightings have been limited to certain colonial-era buildings on the other side of the country. There would be no apparitions bedecked in tricorns, knee-britches and silk hose that night. Rather, it began with nothing more than a sound.

"There was this weird swishing sound," Jason says. "I remember looking at my watch and it was about quarter to 12. At first, I didn't pay it any mind. I was pretty deep into my reading, and I guess it sounded enough like wind in the trees that I didn't think it strange." Even as it got louder, Jason was able to ignore it, assuming that it was just tree boughs on a blustery night.

"I can't remember at exactly what point it hit me that this sound wasn't the wind," he says. "It happened really gradually. I can't even say for sure if it was a matter of the sound getting louder, or just that I was finally paying attention." Sitting up and listening, Jason looked at his watch again. It was just past midnight. "It didn't sound like tree branches to me anymore. I'd describe it as, maybe, nylon swishing together—like someone walking around in nylon pants."

But it was also obvious to Andrews that it *wasn't* someone walking around in nylon pants. "The strangest thing about it was how the volume would fluctuate, like three or four swishes would be faint, like it was coming from far away, and then all of a sudden there would be one swish that was really loud, loud enough to make me jump—as though it was right outside my tent." Jason's first assumption was that his two young charges were goofing on him.

"I called out to my nephew to quit whatever it was that he and his friend thought they were doing," he says. But the swishing continued, unabated. "I called out again, but the sound just kept up. I think that was when it hit that I had no idea what it was, and that maybe my nephew had nothing to do with it." Anyone who's ever heard unfamiliar noises while lying in a tent at night knows that it doesn't take much to get the imagination going. Many more skittish campers will allow themselves to get spooked by the sound of a rolling pebble, or by a prankish camping partner hissing: *Did you hear that?*

Thus, if courage is too strong a word, Jason certainly exhibited an unusual steadiness in his ability to ignore the chill rising up his neck enough to unzip his tent to investigate. "The sound was still going on when I got outside," he says. "I headed straight for my nephew's tent. Their runners were there, right outside their tent, and I could hear them sleeping inside."

Jason continued his investigation. "At first, it seemed to be coming from the lake, so I started out in that direction. It was hard to tell, because the sound was inconsistent. One minute, it'd be kind of loud—like it was really close—then it would sound farther off. When I was walking to the lake, I was starting to get kind of weirded it out. Not *scared*. Just weirded out. I had no idea what I was following," he says. "And this noise, how it was jumping around all over the place. It was like nothing I'd ever heard before. It was unnatural."

As erratic as the sound was, it was constant enough to give Jason the impression that he was getting closer to it as he walked toward the lake. And then it stopped. "This is going to sound out-there, but *that* was when I got scared. The swishy noise was creepy, sure. But it was worse, *way* worse, after it stopped. At that point, I was standing out by the lake, and there was the feeling—this suspicion—that something had *led* me out there. I don't know if it was my mind playing tricks on me or what, but I got hit by this feeling that there was someone there watching me."

Or not quite *someone*. "Actually, if the feeling was that there was someone there, I think I would've said 'who's there' or something. It wasn't like that. It felt more like the *place* was watching me. Like the trees, the lake, like the whole place knew I was there, and was looking." Jason swung his flashlight around, but the more of his surroundings he saw through the thin cone of light, the more the feeling grew.

"I started walking back to the tents, but broke into a run almost right away. I wasn't thinking anything that point. I had no idea what was going on. I just wanted to be back inside my tent." A few minutes later he was in his tent, his heart pounding as he tried to get his head around what had just occurred.

"It took a while, but I started to calm down." And when he did, curiosity began to replace his fear. "I've got to say that I'm not the kind of guy who scares easy," Jason continues. "I know I'd be able to take care of myself in most situations, so there aren't too many things that scare me. I pulled myself together—told myself that whatever happened by the lake, chances are it was just my imagination running a marathon. I made it up. Crazier things have happened."

But there was still the matter of that weird swishing noise, and the further Jason got from it, the more convinced he became that he'd been fooled with. "It wasn't like it was crowded at the park that weekend," he says. Sitting in the dark, looking for an explanation, it didn't take Jason long to come up with his prime suspects. "I know I saw their shoes outside their tent and heard them breathing, but that didn't matter. I asked myself a few 'what-ifs,' and thought that it wouldn't be too hard for them to set this up if they put some planning into it. Believe me—I knew my nephew, and wouldn't put something like this past him."

A shining example of what the mind will tell itself when confronted with the inexplicable, Jason regained his calm, unzipped the tent and headed back out, intending to confront his nephew and his friend about their little prank. He'd just stepped outside and started walking to his nephew's tent when he was stopped in his tracks by a now-familiar feeling.

"I got hit with that chill again, like someone out there was watching." Overcome with the feeling, Jason stopped and shone his light on his nephew's tent. The shoes were still there. Whatever he'd convinced himself of just seconds ago in his tent dissolved once he was outside again. "Sure, the boys could've been fooling around making weird noises and all, but there's no way they were the ones making the hair stand up on my neck. There was something else going on."

That something else came with a whisper, or a series of whispers, Jason isn't clear when he speaks about it. "When I heard the sounds coming from the trees, I wasn't surprised at all. I think I was half expecting it. It was whispering, maybe one person whispering or a bunch of voices at the same time. I'm not sure. I couldn't make out what was being said, but I could hear it clear as anything."

Unlike the swishing noise, Jason was sure the whispering was coming from a definite direction, and promptly went after it. "First I asked who was there, and when the whispering kept up, I decided I was going to get to the bottom of this. That's just my style. I was almost running toward it."

As before, the sounds were leading Jason to the lake, but this time by a different route. "This time, instead of running straight for the lake, I was sort of running toward and along it. The voices were always just ahead of me. I picked up my pace, but it didn't feel like I was getting any closer. And what was really weird is that there was no sound of movement ahead of me. It was just the whispering."

After what Jason describes as a 20 to 30 second blind rush through the bush, "the whispering stopped, just like that." Taking a quick look around with his flashlight, Jason discovered that he was standing right next to the abandoned house he'd seen 100 times over in daylight. "I used to barely notice the place," he says, "but I'll never look at it the same after that night."

To this day, Jason isn't sure if it was knowing that he'd been guided to the house, or just something about the house itself, but he was overcome again with a sense of cold foreboding, and this time it was more powerful than anything he had felt that night. "Basically, I think my body was telling me to get out of there. I had that freezing feeling up my back, and my stomach was queasy."

Though not a man prone to fear, Jason knew there was only one thing to do at that point. "So I ran back for the tent as fast as I could in the darkness." Only once did his footing fail him as he stumbled and fell over an unseen dip in the ground. "That was the only time I looked over my shoulder at the house." Jason stops for a brief moment, and he's obviously unsure about what he's about to say. "I can't say I'm 100 percent about this, because it was dark and I was running and kinda scared, but right then, I swore I saw someone, or more like the shape of someone. A black silhouette of a man standing in front of the house."

That would essentially conclude Jason's adventures that evening. While no other sounds bothered him from within his tent for the rest of the night, he didn't get a single minute of sleep, wired as he was. "I kept replaying what happened over and over in my head, but by the time the boys were up, it dawned on me that I wasn't about to say a word to them. I've told a few people since then, but for the most part, I've kept what happened that night under my hat."

What were the noises about? And who was the man in front of the house? Preliminary research revealed very little about any haunting in Bonito Park. Though it appears there have been some stories about an abandoned house on Bonito Lake, with inexplicable flashes of light and noises coming from within, the goings-on there are definitely not among the most talked about supernatural phenomena in New Mexico. It is a lesser known haunting, still waiting to be corroborated by more campers—campers such as Jason, who actually go out and investigate those strange noises outside their tents.

A Visitation in the Wilderness

Up until that first night out, it had been a camping trip like any other. Our camper, who shall go by the pseudonym of Pedro Lehrman, was out in the Edward Sargent State Wildlife Area in northwestern New Mexico, tramping through the lush and rugged land. "Hiking has always been one of my favorite things to do," Lehrman says. "I've been doing it ever since my dad bought me my first pair of hiking boots for my 15th birthday."

Happiest when following a trail through forests and rocky peaks, Lehrman says he has hiked different terrains all over the world. "I'd say I've been to quite a few places. I've hiked in Scotland, the Swiss Alps, the Canadian Rockies and once in Nepal. Here in the States, I've been all the way up and down the Divide, from Montana down south to the border, but in my opinion, there's nothing as beautiful to me as the landscape of New Mexico."

Granted, Lehrman is not able to claim a freedom from bias. "This was the wilderness that I grew up with," he continues. "My family didn't live in New Mexico, but my dad and big brother were both into camping, and this was their favorite country to hike in. When I was a kid, we'd make the drive across the border for summer expeditions. I never really got over it. Wherever I go, I'm always making comparisons with New Mexico, and in my mind, nothing else really added up."

Lehrman had no reason to believe that the trip he was planning to the Edward Sargent Wildlife Area on that July weekend was going to be different from any other he'd embarked upon. His brother and best friend had both backed out at the last minute, so he was going to be camping alone, but he'd done that many times before and didn't think twice about it. In fact, this time around, he was looking forward to the solitude.

"Me and my wife had just split a few months ago, and at the time, I knew I wouldn't be the best company. I think I was a little bit let down when I first found out that my brother and friend couldn't make it out, but the more I thought about being on my own, the better I felt about it. I knew I needed to be alone. That's how I've always sorted things out—with peace and quiet and a good chunk of alone time."

Surely there was no better place for him to enjoy some solitude. "I'd camped at Sargent before," he says, "so it wasn't like I was getting into anything new." Lehrman pauses for a moment, and when he continues his voice is slightly lower. "I ought to say, as well, that this was the first place I ever went camping as a kid. My dad used to take us, me and my brother. We spent a lot of summer weekends out there. Those were some of my best childhood memories."

Lehrman says that his nostalgia for the wildlife area has always resonated deeply with him, and that he always leaves feeling undeniably rejuvenated and peaceful. This trip, however, would be much different. "First day was just like any other, I guess. No one was staying at my favorite campsite, so I grabbed it quick. It's always the same, the way the fresh air hits me when I step out of the truck. I've always felt totally at home in northern New Mexico."

"As far as popular attractions go, there's nothing really that flashy about the Sargent area. None of those spectacular vistas that draw in the big crowds. The campsites are actually quite bare. There are easier places for people to camp. I mean, this place doesn't dress itself up for visitors all that much. But that's just the way I like it."

After setting up camp in the early afternoon, Lehrman spent the rest of the day wandering around, taking in the hills, forests and water, allowing himself to readjust to the quiet rhythms of the area. He emphasizes that everything was as he remembered it, and he became nostalgic, remembering all the trips he took with his father and brother. While he was still lost in his memories, he lit a fire and cooked his dinner, watching the sky change color as the sun dipped out of sight. It was then, as the first stars appeared, that Lehrman felt it for the first time.

"I still don't know how to explain it, exactly," he says. "One second, I was sitting there, remembering some of the stories my dad would tell me and my brother when we were sitting around the fire, and then everything *changed*." Lehrman continues: "I don't know what to say except that I was sure I wasn't alone anymore. It was like there was someone with me, right there, enjoying the fire, the stars and the peace and quiet." Lehrman then says that he felt a strange warm rush come over him, and he just smiled.

Some might call this an odd reaction. A solitary man in the wilderness sitting before a fire at night is overcome by an undeniable feeling that he is not alone, that something near and unseen is sitting there with him, and he smiles? He feels comforted? When Lehrman is confronted by this question, he has trouble explaining exactly what he was feeling. "I know I should've been unsettled by it, but it's hard to explain. I was just feeling comfortable with it, and I guess I didn't really have any control over what I was feeling. I *knew*

Pedro was looking forward to the solitude.

there was something out there, and I *knew*, whatever it was, that it was friendly."

Lehrman falls back on his Christian beliefs. "I am a man of faith, so maybe that had something to do with the way I felt. Sure, some people are going to get scared in a situation like that—because they don't know what they're dealing with. Me, I've got a belief in God." He pauses and adds with a laugh, "and I know that I'm in with Him. Like they say, if you're in with the Lord, you've got nothing to worry about. God works in mysterious ways, I suppose, and my thinking was that night, he was working on me."

Lehrman felt the troubles that had been plaguing him suddenly dissolve. "At the time, I'd been torturing myself about my ex-wife. It was like my head was on a treadmill or something. I was in that mindset where I was asking myself the same questions over and over again. Questions like: Was it my fault? Could I've done something different? Will I be alone for the rest of my life?"

Yet while in the presence of what Lehrman assumed was some divine force, the treadmill just stopped. For the first time in months, he was able to think past these questions. "Talking about this, I have to get across that I'm thinking along the lines of miracles here. I mean, that's what it felt like. Like there was an actual weight off my shoulders. Right then, I literally felt lighter. I remembered what it was like to be a kid again, sitting in front of a campfire without a care in the world."

Though not everyone will remember childhood in such ideal terms, this is the way Lehrman recalls it. And sitting there, in the perceived presence of a higher, beneficent force, he felt as though he was traveling back to that time in his life—as though he were a child again, camping with his father. It was a feeling that would grow evermore concrete as his time in the bush went on.

"I'm not sure how long I sat there that night," he says. "All I can say for sure is that I said goodnight to the fire pit before I hit the sack, and that I fell asleep with a smile on my face." Lehrman spent the next day hiking, the good energy from the night before carrying into the next day.

"That night, I grabbed a chair and headed out to one of my favorite vistas in the area to watch the sun go down. The sunset was as incredible as I remembered it, and I started thinking about my ex-wife. I'd brought her out there a few times, when things had been good. Then I remember thinking about how it went wrong—whose fault it was and all that. That she was mad, sure. But you know, I had just as much right to be angry." But before he was able to go far down the same road of recrimination and guilt that he had set upon so many times before, Lehrman's "miracle" returned.

He describes it as the feeling from the night before, except stronger. "It started the same. I knew for a fact that I wasn't alone, and whatever was there with me was friendly. This time, though, it felt much closer, like it was right beside me, and when I looked over, there was a second when I swore for a second that I saw it. Or him, I should say. It was a hazy outline of a tall man with big shoulders. He didn't have any features. All that was there was a misty outline that looked kind of orange in the sunset. It was there for a second, and then it was gone," Lehrman says.

Yet though the wispy vision had vanished from sight, the feeling of warmth and comfort remained. It was so tangible that Lehrman looked over and said hello. When the presence replied, he nearly jumped out of his chair. "The fact that a voice said 'hi' back was strange enough, but what really got to me was that the voice was *familiar*. I'd heard it before. I mean, it sounded far away and there was this echo. But the voice itself, I knew I'd heard it a thousand times, I just couldn't figure out *where*."

Then it spoke again. "It said: 'Set yourself free. Everything's going to be okay.' I didn't know what to say to that," Lehrman continues, "but everything felt better. The anger about my ex was gone, just like that, and I didn't feel guilty either. The voice had just told me to set myself free, and right then, that's pretty well how I felt. It was great."

Lehrman goes on to say that he ended up sitting there in the darkness well after the sun had gone down, knowing that he was not alone and feeling glad about it, and sure that he was almost ready to move on past his failed marriage. Indeed, the events that were to transpire later that night would finally relegate his ex-wife to little else than a memory.

"I'm not the kind of person who usually remembers my dreams, but I'll never forget the one I had that night," Lehrman says. "I was a kid again, and it was just me and my dad. It was a real sunny day and we were camping at Sargent. I remember it feeling great. But then I looked up at my dad, and I got scared. He was staring down at me, like he was worried about something I didn't understand. I remember asking him what was wrong, and he put his hand on my shoulder. It was freezing cold—I mean so cold that it kind of hurt. I still remember it so clearly. He said: 'You know, son, I never told you, but I'm so proud of you. You're a good and decent man, and even when I'm gone, I'll be watching over you. Never forget.'"

Lehrman was wide-awake in a shot, lying in the darkness of his tent, the pressure of his father's hand still hard on his shoulder. All at once, he knew whose voice he had heard at sunset. It had been his father's—strangely distorted, muted as though speaking from a great distance—but his father's nonetheless. Quick on the heels of this realization came the now familiar sense that he was not alone. This time, however, the feeling left him cold and empty—and afraid.

"I think it took a few seconds to sink in, but it hit me that there was someone else in the tent with me, and when I looked over, there was this big black figure lying there, not a foot away. All I could see was his outline against the tent, and it freaked me right out." Lehrman shot up in his sleeping bag and reached for his flashlight. He fumbled for the power button, clicking it desperately several times, but nothing was happening; the light wouldn't switch on. And the figure was still there, right next to him, close enough to touch.

"It was freezing cold in the tent by then," Lehrman says. "As much as I wanted to get out of there, I'd have to reach across the figure to get to the tent zipper, and I just couldn't get myself to do it. I was actually pressed against the opposite side of the tent, as far away as I could get."

According to Lehrman, the figure then spoke, sounding again as though it was somehow coming from a great distance, even though the figure was right there in the tent. And it was the same voice he had heard earlier that night, the voice he had heard in his dream: his father's voice. "He said the same things as before. First about setting myself free, and that he was proud and that he would be looking over me, no matter what. The thing was that this time it was scaring the daylights out of me. My dad was doing great last time I saw him in Colorado. He was a big healthy guy who loved football, camping and his family. He had a loud laugh. I think that was the main reason I didn't recognize his voice earlier. He just wouldn't talk like this. It wasn't him."

Lehrman wasn't able to produce even a word when the figure reached forward and put a hand on his shoulder. The touch was as cold as he remembered it in his dream. "He told me to remember what he said," Lehrman says. "He also said that he loved Mom and my brother, and also that he was waiting." And that was it. Lehrman blinked once and the black silhouette that had been in his tent was gone, the cold numbness on his shoulder the only evidence that he was there at all.

"I didn't sleep again that night, and as soon as the sun came up, I was packing up my stuff and heading home as fast as I could go. I was worried to death about my dad. I mean, I can't say I knew what the heck was going on, but it seemed pretty obvious to me that the night before was some kind of goodbye." He claims that though he understood it on some level, he still wasn't able to accept it. "I know I'd heard stories like this, where the spirits say 'bye' to the people they loved before they die, but even though I believe in God, spirits and a life after death, I just couldn't believe that anything had happened to my dad."

But his worst fears were realized later that day, when he got home and made a call to his parents' home. His aunt answered the phone; she told him that his mother and brother were at the hospital, where his father had been in critical condition for the last two nights, after suffering a massive stroke. His mother had told his aunt to stay at home so that there would be someone there when Pedro called.

He rushed to the hospital as soon as he hung up, arriving at the hospital just in time to see his unconscious father take his last breaths. "Everyone was torn apart, crying. My brother had to leave the room, but it was different for me. Right there, I knew exactly what happened. My dad's spirit visited me before he'd passed to make sure that I'd be okay. He knew that I was having a hard time dealing with my divorce, and at that time losing him would be almost more than I could take. He came by to tell me that he was still around and that everything was going to work out, and that made all the difference."

Today, Lehrman is happily married with two children who he already takes camping. He has learned to look back fondly on that July weekend in the Sargent Wildlife Area, considering himself lucky to have had some final moments with his father. "I know that a lot of folks out there don't get to experience last visits like the one I got, and I don't take it for granted. I thank my dad for those visits almost everyday, and I'm certain that he can hear me. When I look back, the only thing I regret was being so scared, and not saying goodbye properly," Lehrman says. "No problems, I guess I'll just have to explain myself when I finally see him again."

Not Just Another Apartment Suite

Charles Masters (a pseudonym, by request) doesn't live in Santa Fe anymore, and though he says his memories of the picturesque city are mostly fond ones, the ones that will stick occurred when he was alone at home. It was an innocuously modern apartment with a big bright living room and new hardwood floor. Indeed, Masters assumed that the temporary home he was moving into was entirely unexceptional— a fact that he had very little issue with. "I moved to Santa Fe knowing that my work term there was temporary," Masters says. "All I was after was a clean, no-hassles place for one year, two, tops. The apartment building was pretty new, modern-looking, and about as generic a living space as you could imagine." No dark history. No cobwebs, rickety stairs or creaking floorboards. In short, not the sort of residence one might imagine when thinking of haunted dwellings. But in the case of Masters' Santa Fe condo, looks proved to be deceiving.

"I was spending a lot of time at home when I first moved into town," Masters says. "I didn't know too many people in town, and most nights after work, I ended up renting movies or watching TV."

He began noticing strange phenomena almost as soon as he was settled. "I didn't think too much of it at first," Masters says. "It's funny, the things that were happening at first were weird enough to notice, but not really get worried about." He makes a point of describing some of the things that caught his attention. "When I think back, it's completely possible that other weird things might've been happening. I can remember little things that made me think twice: the two towels on the rack in the bathroom had a way of folding themselves; sometimes a glass, dish or fork that I swore I washed and put away would show up in the sink. All kinds of little things that make you wonder if you're getting forgetful or crazy or whatever else."

Masters managed to avoid dwelling on these incidents, attributing them to his own absentmindedness. Then there was the night when something came to life in his bedroom, and everything changed. "I can still remember it really clearly. It was a Saturday in June, and I was at home alone watching a movie on TV. Just another night in my new place. No big deal." And no warning, either.

People who speak of having paranormal experiences often describe a feeling of foreboding that directly precedes the event—a sudden rush of cold, an inexplicable sense of dread, goose bumps, neck hairs standing on end. Masters, however, did not have the benefit of a warning. "One second, I was sitting there, watching this movie, the next, all hell was breaking loose in my bedroom down the hall."

The first crash was loud enough to make him jump. "I was on my feet in a second and running down the hall," Masters says. "At first I was thinking that I hadn't put something together right, maybe my bed or the wardrobe or something had fallen apart. But then there was another crash even before I made it to the bedroom, and I got a bit spooked. Right before I opened the door, I remember wondering if somebody had broken into my apartment." Not quite somebody, it turned out, but some*thing*.

Swinging open his bedroom door, Masters was only able to gape in shock at the sight in front of him. "It still spooks me when I think about it. Two of the drawers from my dresser were on the ground on the other side of the room, and all the clothes that'd been in them were flying in these circles—like someone had set loose a miniature cyclone in there."

The chaos intensified right before Masters' eyes. "I've got four drawers in my dresser. Two were out on the ground, but the other two were still where they belonged. Maybe about 10 seconds after I opened the door, another drawer went flying out of the dresser and crashed into the opposite wall with this crash. The clothes inside of it didn't have a chance to hit the ground though, they just flew into the air and joined the mini-cyclone swirling around all over the place."

That was when Masters decided he had had enough. Whatever was going on in his room, he didn't want any part of it. "I didn't wait around too much longer than that. I slammed the door shut and pretty well ran out of my apartment." What does one do when a scene from *Poltergeist* is being played out in one's room?

"Well, you can't really call the fire department, can you?" Masters says. "I've never been a religious guy, or anyone who believes in ghosts or anything, either. I had no clue. I ended up going for a really long walk around my neighborhood, trying to get my head around whatever the hell just happened." Masters staggered about in disbelief for well over an hour, and it was past midnight by the time he gathered the courage to go back home.

"It took me a while to unlock the door and go inside. The TV was on, and this spooked me at first, until I realized that

I'd left it on when I left. That's the way it was everywhere in all the other rooms, too—exactly like I left it. Except for the bedroom." It was the last room Masters checked, and he opened the door slowly, frightened at what he might find.

"It was pretty much a disaster," he says. "My clothes weren't flying around all over the place anymore, but they were lying around all over the place. All the drawers were on the floor, and my dresser was knocked over, lying on its side." Masters didn't have to deliberate for very long before resolving that there was no way he was going to sleep in his room that night—or, for that matter, any time soon. "I guess I'm lucky that I had a hide-a-bed in the living room," says Masters, " 'cause I ended up getting good use of it." Indeed, this occasion wasn't the last time he found himself barring his bedroom door and opting to sleep on his living room couch.

Over the next few days Masters was so stressed out about whatever had happened that night repeating itself, he gave no thought to what, if anything, he would tell other people regarding the matter. That was something that just decided itself. "The first person to ask me about it was one of the other tenants in the building. This guy lived down the hall from me, and I ran into him two mornings after the night when all hell broke loose in my bedroom. It was a new building, and the suites were pretty well soundproofed, but I guess not soundproofed enough, 'cause when we were making small talk in the stairwell he asked me what the racket was in my place the night before.

"I made up a story without even thinking about it," Masters says. "I told him that I was hammering some furniture together. I don't know if he believed me or not, but he let it go at that." Masters did not tell anyone about the phenomena occurring in his apartment the entire time he was living there. "Thinking back, it's funny how I kept it like some sort of dirty secret. It wasn't like I was thinking that it was my fault or something, but I was kind of embarrassed about it. I guess it makes sense that I wouldn't tell my coworkers, none of whom I really knew too well. But I didn't tell my friends and family back home, either." Was it simply a matter of embarrassment? Concern that his friends and family would think he was losing his mind? Or was he himself concerned that he might be losing his mind? "I still don't know what to say about it. I once told a friend while drinking, and then after I was done, I told him that I was just pulling his leg. What can I say?" Apparently, as long as his identity remains confidential, Masters is ready to say a lot. The years of silence seem to have led to an irrepressible need to talk.

"It wasn't just the bedroom, but that's definitely where most of the stuff went on," he continues. "After that first time, there was something weird going on in my room almost every night. Mostly it wasn't too crazy—nothing like what happened with my dresser drawers. Usually I'd hear a thump, and go in to see a chair, a lamp or my alarm clock lying on the ground. Also, when the light was off in the hallway, there were times when I could see the lights strobing on and off from under the doorway. Every time, I went for the doorknob to see, but by the time I opened it, the lights were off."

For the most part, the phenomena were tame enough, and although he now slept in his living room, he was able to live a mostly normal life. "Not that it was smooth sailing or anything. There were some nights when things in the bedroom went completely nuts all over again."

Masters describes the night he woke up to the sound of his bedroom door slamming shut over and over again. "I turned on the lights and saw it, the door opening by itself really slowly, then slamming shut hard." He solved the problem that night by duct taping pillows against the doorway.

"There was another night when I actually heard footsteps in the bedroom," Masters says. "They sounded loud, like someone big was moving around fast." This incident stands out in Masters' mind, as it was the first hint of something *real* in his room—there were footsteps, whatever in there was making noise, and for once, it sounded human. "That time, I remember running to my room, really excited, that I was finally going to see this thing that was trashing my room."

While Masters did indeed get quite the eyeful on this occasion, it answered none of his questions. "I felt the cold when I was halfway down the hall—it was this intense cold that went right up my back. It made the hairs on my arms and my neck stand straight up." Masters kept going, throwing open his bedroom door only to be confronted by another mind-boggling sight. "There wasn't a person there. It was a cloud of grayish mist, about six feet tall and maybe four feet wide, moving from one side of my bed to the other." Masters goes on to say that this mist hovered in his room for no more than one or two minutes before dissipating into nothingness. The entire time the mist was in his room, the cold that had seized him did not let up, and even intensified in those few short moments that the mist moved toward him. And it was then, after the vaporous cloud vanished, that Masters confronted the reality of his situation—he was dealing with something beyond his experience, and he wanted to move out of his apartment because of it.

Not that he left in any big rush. In fact, Masters ended up living with the spirit for the better part of six months. "Well, there was the matter of the lease," he says, "but also, weird as it sounds, I just didn't have it in me to pack up and move again, so soon after moving everything in. As creepy as this thing was, it really hadn't done anything to me, besides keep me from a bit of sleep."

And so it was that Masters ended up spending half a year with an active spirit, without the inclination to talk to anyone about what was going on, nor the energy to just get up and leave. "So I toughed it out. But really, it wasn't as bad as you might think. I'm convinced that if you give yourself enough time, you'll be able to get used to anything—even living with a half-crazed spirit that won't leave you alone."

After six months, Masters' apartment was itself a testament to man's ability to adapt. "I guess it's a good thing that I didn't make any close friends in town then," he says, "because I have no idea what someone would think if they came in and saw how I was living." Masters describes a living space that would indeed be fitting for a lunatic: pillows duct-taped to his bedroom doorframe to muffle slamming doors; his dresser relocated to the living room to prevent the thing in the bedroom from throwing around the drawers; the sofa in his living room permanently opened up into bed-mode, where he slept for most of the time he was there; and his dress shirts removed from his bedroom closet now hung from the curtain rods in the kitchen and living room.

Yet even with such precautions, Masters often found himself dealing with disturbing incidents. "Even though it was mostly in my bedroom, every now and then things would happen in other parts of the apartment," he says. "About three or four times a month, stuff in the kitchen would move around by itself. I could always hear it over the TV. Sometimes it was cutlery sliding across the counter. Sometimes the cupboards opened and closed." After a while, Masters didn't even bother to get up and take a look when it happened. "Actually, half the time, I barely noticed it. It got so the only time I got up and fixed things in the kitchen was when I could see a light shine in the hall. That meant that it had opened the fridge."

Masters eventually concluded that there were only two hard rules that dictated his resident spirit's behavior: one, that it seemed to prefer his bedroom, and two, that though it would venture out of his bedroom fairly regularly, it would never initiate anything in a room that Masters happened to be in. "That was the main thing I noticed. Nothing ever happened in the room that I was in. When I was watching TV, cutlery would slide around in the kitchen or footsteps would bang around in my bedroom. But if I was cooking, that's when the TV would flick on and off by itself, or the magazines would fly off my end tables."

And what was this spirit about, exactly? Was this harassment an attempt to say something? Could it have been unhappy about Masters' presence? Or perhaps it was a tortured spirit coping with unhappy circumstances of its demise. "I did try finding out a bit about the place," Masters says. "I never went out of my way or anything, but I managed to ask three other people who lived in the building if they knew anything about who was living in my suite before."

In a way, the answers Masters got were almost as puzzling as the phenomena. "They all said the same thing. It was a pretty new building, and the only person who lived there before me was a single woman. They told me she looked like she could have been somewhere in her mid-30s, tall and good-looking they said, really quiet, and that she lived there for less than one year."

Masters' inability to let on that anything was wrong prevented him from getting any more detail, but it was apparent that there was no known tragic event that had occurred in his apartment suite. No one was murdered, or died of natural causes. The man next door, who had heard the banging in Masters' bedroom, said nothing of any kind of violent relationship or loud rows. The only thing that was slightly unusual was the short duration of the woman's stay, but even that wasn't really so strange, especially given how long Masters was planning on staying.

"I ended up leaving as soon as my lease ran out," he says. "I was really curious about what the super's reaction would be—if he would've been surprised that I was leaving so soon, or if he knew about what was going on there." The enigma only deepened when the superintendent greeted the news with a single, expressionless question: "Weren't too happy with the place?"

To this day, Masters has no idea what to make of his experience in that Santa Fe apartment. "It's definitely changed the way I look at things, that's for sure," he says. "Ghosts and spirits and all that never really did anything for me before. I always thought it was all a load of bunk, and didn't even have it in me to sit through a horror movie. But you go through something like that, and how can you not wonder about it?

No one can tell me now that there's no such thing as ghosts. Or that some part of us doesn't keep living after we're gone."

Not that the time he spent with the mysterious spirit has made him vocal about such matters, or given him any sort of theory about the afterlife. Indeed, if Masters might have scoffed about spiritual topics before, he goes on to say that he's more likely to clam up now if the subject comes up. "It's the way I am," Masters says. "I don't know if I'm embarrassed about it, or worried that people will think I'm nuts, or what. I've just kept my mouth shut about it. This is the first time I've told anyone."

The Evil Under the Bed

Lisa's parents stood by her bedside, looking down at their daughter in dismay. Her arms and legs were strapped to the emergency room bed, but she was not struggling like she had been mere minutes ago. One of the nurses had just injected her with a full dose of morphine, and she was staring up through half-closed eyes, muttering incoherently at the ceiling.

The year was 1943, and the small family was in the emergency room of the Albuquerque Veterans Hospital. They were there because they were desperate. Things had been getting progressively worse for the last two months—their daughter's behavior was getting more and more unsettling, more and more out of control. Finally, on this night, with their daughter babbling incoherently as if possessed, they panicked and brought her to the emergency ward.

It had begun innocently enough. Lisa's parents assumed it was just a dream, or perhaps an overactive imagination, when she woke them in the middle of the night talking about a whimpering puppy in her room. There were no pets in the house, but Lisa's mother went to check her room anyway, making a show out of inspecting inside her closet, under her bed and any other place that a puppy might be. She assured her daughter then that she had looked everywhere, and there was no sign of a dog. She must have been dreaming.

But it soon became clear that if the whimpering pup was indeed a dream, it was a recurring one. There would be no more peaceful evenings in the household; night after night, the whining puppy returned to Lisa's room. The teenager quickly discovered that her parents had very limited patience where invisible puppies whining in the middle of the night were concerned. Waking them up about a dream was one thing, but keeping the whole family up with an overactive imagination fell too close to mischief. Lisa was told to quit the nonsense with a whining puppy, and just go to sleep.

So it was that the teenager stopped disturbing her parents with her late-night visits. And yet the whimpering animal continued to visit her. Every night, she was woken by the sound of piteous whimpers from somewhere in the darkness. It was the sound of a distressed pup, and young Lisa, puzzled and concerned, spent hours every night searching every space in her room, calling out into the darkened corners.

But it was to no avail. Her efforts only led to bleary-eyed days and a growing obsession with the mysterious animal in her room. Futile as her nocturnal searches for the pup were, she never stopped looking. Her parents could hear her searching through her room at night, calling out for her imaginary puppy. They quickly grew concerned.

Not only was Lisa too old to invent an imaginary friend at 15 years of age, but it was also strange that she would choose to make up a companion that caused her so much grief. No matter how much Lisa called for her imaginary pup, she never received a reply. She only heard constant whimpering, pathetic and pleading.

Hoping that she would stop obsessing if left alone, Lisa's parents stood by as their daughter became fixated with helping the invisible dog in her room. It only got worse. The ceaseless whimpering took a heavy toll on the young girl. She was possessed by a need to help the animal, but not being able to see it, there was nothing she could do. She cried late into the night. Her parents could hear her through the walls, calling for the pup that wasn't there. Many times her calls became desperate shouts or wails.

Her parents would burst into her room in the middle of the night to find her digging through her laundry hamper, or else frantically pulling out her dresser drawers, looking for the animal amid a pile of clothes. They tried to get their daughter out of her room, but she refused. It got to the point where she almost never left her room. Afraid that the pup might appear while she was gone, she began having her dinner in her room. She didn't even leave to bathe. Her room became a shambles. She stopped going to school. Lisa's entire life was centered on finding the pup in her room—an animal her parents were convinced she had dreamed up.

Continuing to hope that Lisa would get over the imaginary creature with time, her parents did nothing. Then came the morning when they discovered her sleeping under her bed. She told her parents that she had heard a man's voice that night, telling her that the puppy would come to her if she slept under the bed. First whimpering pups, now a whispering man—Lisa's parents decided then that it was time to get her professional help.

The diagnosis was schizophrenia, but the prescribed medication did nothing for her symptoms. In fact, it wasn't long after Lisa's mother forced the first pill down her daughter's throat that things got out of control. What little there was of the girl her parents knew dissolved completely. The nocturnal hunts for the invisible pup were now punctuated by ear-splitting screams that filled the house throughout the night. Her terrified parents would run into her room to find her frothing at the mouth and swearing viciously in a voice that was not her own.

Obviously, the medication was not working, but when Lisa began reciting the "Our Father" prayer backwards, her parents began to suspect that she might be beyond the help of modern medicine. At one point, her father grabbed her by the shoulders and shook her, begging her to stop. Falling silent at the sight of her father's tear-streaked face, the bedraggled girl stared him in the eyes for a moment before producing a booming, maniacal laugh. Panic descended then; the deep, throaty sound could never have come from the mouth of a 15-year-old girl. Lisa was no longer their daughter. There was something else inside her, something beyond their control. Their panic took them straight to the emergency room at the Albuquerque Veterans Hospital, where their daughter was promptly bound to a bed and filled with morphine. Lisa's parents were standing over her bed when, for the first time, they thought of resorting to more divine forces for aid. They asked the nurses if it was possible for them to see a priest.

A recently ordained Catholic priest, Father Henry was the pastor at the hospital, trusted to celebrate Mass with the patients and staff. He was doing his rounds among the patients when a nurse approached him with Lisa's story, telling him how her parents believed her to be under the control of some evil force. Minutes later he was in the emergency room with the distressed family, listening to the parents' tearful account of the last several weeks.

A young priest confident in the power of his faith, Father Henry did not hesitate for a moment. If this girl was indeed possessed by an evil force, a blessing from his God would surely drive this force away. Assuring Lisa's parents that everything was going to be fine, he went straight to his office to retrieve a vial of holy water. A blessing was what he had in mind, but when he appeared back at the doorway, it was immediately clear that Lisa, or, rather, the evil force inside her was not at all eager to receive such a blessing.

She began to shriek when he appeared in the doorway, snapping from her drug-induced tranquility in an instant. "Get away from me!" she screamed, straining against her bonds. "Don't take a step closer!"

Father Henry stopped, taken aback at the violence of her reaction. But her parents, beyond desperation, urged him to come forward. Now convinced there was an evil in their daughter that needed to be confronted, they looked to the priest with newfound hope; this ordained man was just the man to help Lisa. Father Henry's experience is recounted in Antonio Garcez's *Adobe Angels: The Ghosts of Albuquerque*.

"I decided to do a simple blessing over the child," he says. "I unscrewed the bottle containing the holy water and placed a few drops on my hand." Reciting a prayer, he stepped forward and pressed his wet palm over Lisa's forehead.

She began screaming as soon as he touched her: "Stop! You're killing me! You're killing me, you son of a bitch!" Even her parents started at the horror in their daughter's voice.

Shocked at the outburst, Father Henry yanked back his hand, even as the words began to spill from his mouth. "Child, be at peace with your Savior who will deliver you."

Lisa opened her eyes then, and the look in them was like a physical blow. Father Henry stepped back, shaken to the core, terrified at the evil in those glaring brown eyes. Still, he continued: "The love of our Father in heaven and of his own son Jesus Christ bless you."

Bedlam followed. Letting out a terrible scream, Lisa broke free from her bonds. Her parents and the priest backed away slowly, staring agape at the possessed girl. Several nurses had also rushed into the room, but halted at the sight on the bed. Lisa was babbling now, a jumble of meaningless sounds spilling from her mouth, her expression going back and forth from maniacal joy to utter despair. No one, not even the nurses, dared step forward.

Wide-eyed and grinning, she clasped one of her feet as her incoherent babble turned into a ceaseless mantra. "Jesus loves me," she said. "Jesus loves me. Jesus loves me." Over and over again she said the words. Her hands gripped her foot tightly now, then pulled back toward her with such force that the bones dislocated and snapped. The sound of her breaking bones filled the room, yet Lisa gave no sign of pain, her grin only widening as she pulled back harder.

Another bone broke, and they acted. Father Henry lunged forward with Lisa's father. "We took hold of her arms and pulled with all our might," Father Henry would later say. "Her strength was unbelievable!"

Lisa's mother shouted at Father Henry to continue with the religious ritual, ordering him to douse her daughter with holy water. The nurses grabbed the limb the priest had been holding onto while he unscrewed the bottle and emptied it on the thrashing girl. She let out a frightful wail, a tortured, high-pitched scream that sent everyone in the room reeling back.

That was when the unthinkable occurred. One of the nurses let out a scream as an enormous black dog bounded out from under Lisa's hospital bed. The sight of such a lumbering animal in the sterile hospital room was a complete shock. Father Henry, Lisa's parents and the nurses could only stand and stare, paralyzed in wonder, as the dog bolted out the door.

The screams in the hallway brought two of the nurses back to their senses, and they promptly ran out after the dog, gathering a group of other employees as they did so. Yet somehow, the big black canine was never found. It was there one moment, loping down one of the long, white halls. Then it turned a corner and was gone. No one could explain it. There was no exit in the hallway, and the doors along the walls, all closed, could not be opened unless someone turned the handles—something that a dog would obviously not be able to do. The enormous animal had just vanished.

As for Lisa, the moment the dog dashed out from under her bed, the diabolical fire in her eyes went out. All at once, she was a teenage girl again—albeit a terrified, confused and exhausted teenage girl. Looking around the hospital room with bewildered eyes, she reached out and began to sob the moment she saw her mother, and the two embraced before the relieved crowd that had gathered in the emergency room with the family. After spending one night under observation in the hospital, Lisa was released. She was ragged and had her foot in a cast, but was on her way to a full recovery.

Father Henry goes on to say that he stayed in contact with Lisa and her parents for some time. "She turned out to be as normal as can be," he said. Her memories of the experience faded rapidly in the years that followed. No more whining puppies were to be heard in her room, and the black dog that had emerged from under the hospital bed was never seen again. With any luck, it knew its way home and stayed put once it got there.

Highway 666:
What's in a Name?

I'm pleased that after years of controversy, this issue, which has plagued the Navajo Nation and Northwestern New Mexico, has finally been resolved.

—*Bill Richardson, Governor of New Mexico*

The Governor's office made it public on June 5, 2003. The New Mexico Highway and Transportation Department had finally renamed its most notorious stretch of road. U.S. 666 was no longer. The 200-mile highway, running from Monticello, Utah, through to Gallup, New Mexico, would be purged of its ominous three digits. Roughly $10,000 of state money would be spent to replace every sign stamped with the Revelator's number of the Beast, putting up innocuous U.S. 491 signs in its place. Highway 666, also known as the road of the dead, Devil's Highway, Satan's Speedway and the Highway to Hell, had spawned far too many bizarre legends, offended far too many religious sensibilities. So it was that the 666 became the 491, and a number of the United States' most lasting and most bizarre folktales were laid to rest. Or were they?

In the beginning, it was the science in the system, not the devil in the machine, which allowed Highway 666 to exist. It was a purely secular numbering system, developed by the United States' Joint Board on Interstate Highways, not the biblical prophesies written in the Book of Revelation, which lent this lonesome road its controversial handle. Nevertheless, all the horrific tales that sprouted up about this asphalt thoroughfare seem to affirm the opposite when the years brought a legion of demented stories that were saturated with incredible terrors and atrocities. Satan's Speedway earned an unfounded reputation as the deadliest road in the United States. The dead were said to be heaped along its shoulders: the angry and vengeful dead, whose souls mingled with phantom rigs, ravaging hellhounds and the vehicle of none other than the Devil himself—Satan's Sedan, speeding over the silver landscape at unearthly speeds.

Once upon a time, when Highway 491 was still Highway 666, the author interviewed an anonymous contact about his experiences on the road. He was called "Jordan Ashley," and the following was his story:

"I was driving back home after a business trip to Albuquerque and took the Highway 666 exit off the I40 at Gallup. The sun was just starting to go down when I hit the 666. I've done a lot of driving through New Mexico, so I knew all about the stories. They're everywhere…'Don't drive the 666 at night' they say. Of course, they say the worst thing you can do is drive the road when there's a full moon out. But at the time, I wasn't much of a believer and didn't really think twice at the sight of this big fat orange moon coming up on the horizon.

"Growing up in Utah, I've seen some pretty amazing skies at the end of the day, but I'd *never* seen anything like this before. I mean, these red clouds came out of nowhere, looked like they were ink that was spilled across the sky. And when I

New signage was up along the highway to remind motorists of the official name change.

say they were red, they were really, really red. It looked like the sky was bleeding."

Spectacular as the natural display was, it left Ashley with an inexplicable feeling of dread: "I don't know how to describe it, but it had something to do with this real strong feeling that I didn't *belong* there, on the road. Like the sun was taking forever to set and there was this incredible red light all around, and just the sight of the sky was starting to freak me out. And it wasn't just the sky; the whole desert turned red, everything was different shades of the same color. My stomach started to get really tight, and right then, I just wanted to get out of there as soon as I could."

But there was nowhere else to go. It was nothing but the road and the red horizon, which stretched out before him, a smoldering eternity—until the sun sank out of sight, the full moon rose and all hell broke loose. Quite literally. Two headlights, quite a ways in the distance, appeared behind him.

"I got a lump in my throat the moment I saw those lights in my mirror. There's no reason to get scared of a car coming up behind you, and believe me, I don't normally scare easily, but the sight of this guy's lights put the fear of God in me. I knew then that this situation was no good. A part of me was tempted to turn around and get off the 666, but that would mean driving toward whoever was coming up behind."

He decided his best bet was to put the road behind him as quickly as possible and so he floored the gas pedal. Pushing his vehicle to over 80 miles an hour, he thought he might be able to make it to Monticello within the next hour and a half. And the car behind him, with those headlights that filled him with such inexplicable dread, would soon vanish in the distance. He was wrong.

"I couldn't believe it. I was pushing close to 90 miles per hour in the pitch dark and the car behind me was still getting closer. And he was getting closer *fast*. I know it seems totally impossible, but this car must've been going well over 100 miles per hour. The lights kept getting bigger and bigger in my rearview mirror, until the car was about 50 yards behind me. That's when he put his brights on, and the inside of my car lit up like it was daytime."

Ashley panicked, swerving into the other lane in an attempt to get the car off his back, but the car mirrored his move. A second later, the car was riding his bumper, and Ashley, then desperate, drove his car off the road, skidding out of control as his tires hit dirt. He glanced over at the vehicle as it roared past and could not—did not—believe his eyes. "There was no way a car that big could be going that fast. I couldn't see too clearly in the dark, but I was able to make out that it was a big black sedan…an older car too. Like maybe an early 70s Ford Galaxie or something. It was a boat. What's more, it looked like the car might have been overheating; there was smoke streaming out from under its hood and off the roof. The smoke looked silver in the moonlight."

The startled motorist wasn't able to gawk at this automobile for too long. Plowing over sand and rock off-road, going far too fast for comfort, he tried to get back on the highway but spun out of control when one of his tires went out. The car made a few more wild revolutions before it skidded to a halt in the dirt.

"When the car finally stopped, I didn't slow down for a second. I got out, threw open the trunk and went to work. There was this urgency. I didn't want to be stationary for any longer than I had to. It felt like I was in hostile territory."

Then: "I'd almost finished putting the spare on when the air was filled with the sound of howling. It sounded like they were everywhere, a pack of roving dogs, and though I couldn't see them I knew beyond a shadow of a doubt that they were coming for me."

He left his torn tire lying in the dirt, jumped into his car and roared back onto the road, leaving a cloud of dust behind him. Just as he began to pick up speed he spotted what he swore was over a dozen enormous dogs loping along the road behind him—their eyes shone yellow in the night. Ashley drove the rest of the way as fast as his car could take him, reaching Monticello within the hour, swearing that he would never take the 666 again.

Was Ashley a man with an overactive imagination run off the road by an aggressive driver? Or, perhaps, something else. This was not the only far-fetched story to come from the former Highway to Hell. Ghost lore ran thick over the road, with numerous tales similar to Ashley's. The recurring black automobile was dubbed the "Satan's Sedan." In some accounts, it would come up in the rearview mirror, running drivers off the road and roaring past, while in others, the blinding headlights suddenly appeared head on, playing chicken with horrorstruck commuters, who would unfailingly swerve off the road to get away from the maniacal driver.

There were also the stories of the hounds. Described as a pack of vicious dogs that habitually chased down cars, they were Highway 666's "Hounds of Hell," and were said to be capable of shredding car tires with their teeth or leaping through windshields to maul commuters even as they were driving.

As for those individuals who had the misfortune of being stranded on Highway 666, they were said to be vulnerable to another malevolent vehicle that was said to travel up and down the road. An enormous deep crimson rig was believed to be piloted by a soulless trucker who had a virulent hatred for any living thing that may be on the side of the road. Moving at a phenomenal speed, this trucker made it a habit to plow into anyone who happened to be standing on the shoulder. Legend has it that dozens of hitchhikers met their end on the steaming grill of this massive semi.

On top of all of this, it was also said that there was a ghost—the apparition of a pale young girl who stood very still on the shoulder of the highway, looking deathly pale with long black hair and disturbingly large, lifeless eyes. The girl was said to be barefoot, looking rather fragile, almost pleading, in a white nightgown that hung from her narrow shoulders. Drivers who saw her would pull over, thinking her a distressed youngster in need of help. Yet she would never stick around long enough to answer motorists' concerned queries, usually vanishing into the hot desert air before a person could say: "Where are your parents?"

Where did she go? Indeed, where have all the supernatural beings that once haunted this stretch of road go? Recent research into the highway have revealed an incredible dearth of such accounts, compared to the abundant number of tales that once circulated when the 491 was the 666. It begs the question: What's in a name? Did the Devil and his undead minions only favor the road when the state's highway and transportation department named it after him? Certainly, given the way the tales have dropped off, there was no intrinsic evil imbedded in the land the highway cut through. Were these stories wishful thinking among individuals with morbid imaginations? Or could we be looking at exaggerations of isolated incidents, and concurrent illusions spawned by nothing more than the power of suggestion?

Who can say for sure, and many might say $10,000 is too high a price to pay for the mere purpose of killing such legends and alleviating people's superstitious fears. At least it can be said that now the Devil has no way of getting from Monticello to Gallup, not by way of car, anyway.

5
Other
Restless
Spirits

What Goes On in the Cottonwood Hotel

His name was George Brooks, and he claimed that he was able to speak with the dead. He went some distance on this assertion, making a name for himself as a psychic of a certain distinction among the 19th-century spiritualists in London, England. At the time, London was one of the major centers of paranormal study in the world, and it was on those foggy streets that Brooks developed his connection with the netherworld.

Near the turn of the century, however, Mr. Brooks moved to the still-young city of Los Angeles, where he set himself up as the local expert on matters beyond the grave. He was the southern city's very own Doctor of Divinity, offering up his services to those with the dead on their minds. For a price he directed séances, delivered messages back and forth between the living and the dead, made psychic predictions and investigated potential hauntings on the sunny west coast.

One of Mr. Brooks' regular appointments was in the Verde Valley, Arizona, where he conducted regular lectures and psychic workshops. Whenever he was in this region his preferred residence was the Cottonwood Hotel, in the town of Cottonwood. It was during one such lecture that he made a dire prediction about his favorite town in the Southwest, telling a transfixed audience that the worst disaster in Cottonwood's history would strike that year, 1925. He claimed the message had been passed on to him from the spirit world, and that there was no way of preventing it despite vigilance, doubts or prayers of the populace.

Even the most credulous of his audience would be surprised how immediate Mr. Brooks' prediction came true. The very next night, an explosion rocked the little town when an enormous bootlegging distillery on the west side of town went up in a fiery roar. The blast leveled the town's whole west side and was, just as George Brooks predicted, the worst disaster in Cottonwood's history. Incredibly, the destruction claimed only one person—none other than George Brooks himself, his scorched skeleton found in the rubble of the Cottonwood Hotel.

According to reports, his bones were discovered some distance from his room. Forensics assumed that he'd been trying to get down the corridor when the fire claimed him. But more suspicious minds offered an alternative explanation, citing superstitious townsfolk who never had much love for Mr. Brooks and his public dabbling in spiritual matters. The insinuation was that his final prediction might have frightened certain individuals into action, and that he might have been murdered *before* the explosion ripped through town. This accusation was never substantiated in any way, and it didn't change the fact that George Brooks was now dead— the psychic who was able to forecast the Cottonwood's fiery destruction was ironically unable to read his own demise within it.

The Cottonwood Hotel that stands today was rebuilt on the same site as the original, with pains taken so that it was exactly identical to the place that stood before. And yet, once it was completed, it soon became clear that something had changed. The hotel had acquired a permanent guest, one who never bothered to sign in, and was bent on mischief.

The historic Cottonwood Hotel

From practically the first day the hotel was reopened for business, it was plagued with all sorts of bizarre phenomena. Disembodied footfalls were often heard making their way up and down the halls. Objects in the hotel had an unsettling way of coming to life—combs jumped from dressers, cutlery regularly leapt off tabletops, clothes neatly hung in closets would mysteriously find their way onto bedroom floors while guests were gone. Long before air conditioning was invented, certain rooms and corridors had a way of getting very cold very quickly. Of course, it wasn't long before employees and patrons alike began to talk about George Brooks, the only man who had ever died within its walls, and a spiritualist to boot. Could it be that this man, who had been so preoccupied with the world of the dead while he was alive, had come to haunt the living after death? This popular belief continues to this day.

Indeed, even after all these years, the bizarre happenings at the Cottonwood Hotel still occur. The fact that the Cottonwood is reputed to be haunted by a spirit from its past is actually quite appropriate, considering how rooted the building is in the local history. Not only has the hotel been put on the National Historic Register, but the current ownership has also labeled four of its five rooms after historical figures. There's the John Wayne Suite, the Mae West, the Elvis and, of course, the George H. Brooks Suite.

Oddly enough, of all the rooms, the one that is said to be the site of the *least* ghostly activity is the George H. Brooks Suite. The rebuilt version of the room that Brooks stayed in on the night of his death is almost devoid of unexplainable phenomena. *Almost*, but not entirely. The current owner, Karen Leff, is able to recall one incident where she found a wall ornament turned upside down, though the door had been locked for days and no one had been in the room during that time. Perhaps, then, the ghost of George H. Brooks just rests in his old room and makes mischief through the rest of the building.

Active as the purported spirit is, however, there seems to be very little sense or pattern to the phenomena that are attributed to it. Its activities seem to be focused on different parts of the building at different times. For instance, the spirit seemed to be particularly drawn to the Desert Fury Suite while it was being renovated. All sorts of noises were heard within while the room was locked and empty. During this time, more than one person heard the bed squeaking, a door being opened and shut and the shower running. Footsteps were heard at the oddest hours, pacing back and forth across the room. One guest staying in the room under the Desert Fury went so far as to ask Ms. Leff about the noisy boarder above. We might imagine his surprise when Ms. Leff responded that no one was staying there.

Once renovations were complete, the goings-on in the Desert Fury abated, moving on to other areas in the building. Whether it's a sudden cold spot on the staircase, weird images appearing on photographs taken by patrons or footsteps up and down the corridors, the spirit at the Cottonwood seems to be forever lurking. The premonitions of guests considered to be sensitive to spiritual activity have resulted in the only real theory regarding the phenomena in one of the hallways: that George Brooks is eternally struggling to find his way out of the building as it burns around him.

If he hasn't found his way out by now, it is doubtful that the spirit of Mr. Brooks is ever going to make it out of the Cottonwood Hotel. It's probably a good thing, then, that he isn't making too much of a nuisance of himself, and that the patrons and the proprietor are able to tolerate his continued presence. So it is that the ghost of the Cottonwood remains a constant, if curious, guest at this Arizona hotel.

Japanese Spirits in the Arizona Desert

The Colorado River Indian Reservation extends across the Arizona-California border. Made up of 278,000 acres of spectacular desert and lush, alluvial river bottom lands, the impressive reservation is home to four southwestern Indian nations—the Nu Wu, Mohave, Hopi and Navajo. Yet there was a time when another people also called the reservation home. Unlike the four tribes that occupy the reservation, the fifth group that lived there had no cultural affinity or historical connection to the Arizona desert. Indeed, one would be hard pressed to think of a group more alien to the arid region. They were the American Japanese, and if not for the extreme wartime policy of the United States government during the Second World War, they would never have been there.

With the prospect of war against the Japanese looming in the not-too-distant future, President Franklin Roosevelt passed an executive order that saw tens of thousands of Japanese-Americans in the western United States deported to internment camps. One of these camps was located on the Colorado River Indian Reservation, and so it was that 17,876 American citizens were put on trains and relocated to the reservation between May and August of 1942.

They stayed on for over four years, building their homes in the pagoda style particular to Asian architecture with their own hands using lumber supplied by the government. They raised their families, grew vegetables in community gardens and set up a movie theater—all approximations of normal life as they hoped for a hasty end to the war and wondered if they would ever get their homes back.

It wasn't easy. Most of them had come from California and had long grown accustomed to life on the coast. Here, they were in the middle of the desert, with cruel dust storms, scorching summers and cold, cutting winters. Despite the conditions, life continued on: children were born into these internment camps, while others died there.

Indeed, another stamp of the Japanese forced settlement was the graves they left behind. The cemetery was located in Parker, the biggest town on the reservation. Although many of the elders who were buried there during the internment were disinterred and returned to the West Coast towns they had come from, many others were left behind, resting not-so-peacefully after having died in unjust captivity on American soil.

In 1946, after the internees were released, most of the living quarters they had constructed were disassembled and cut into lumber for the use of the local Indian bands. Still, a few of the Japanese houses were left standing and were given to any Indian families desiring them. And it was the strange goings-on in these homes that gave birth to the tales of the restless dead on the Colorado River Indian Reservation.

In his book, *American Indian Ghost Stories of the Southwest*, Antonio Garcez interviews Betty Cornelius, Director of the Colorado Indian Museum. She comments, "I know of one Indian family that moved into one of those Japanese houses, and they had strange things happen. Doors of the house would open and close on their own. A chair would move away from the table as if pushed by invisible hands—as if someone was about to seat themselves down for

Buildings were constructed for Japanese-American internees at the Colorado River Indian Reservation in 1942.

a meal—the chair would move away from the table, then it would move back against the table! Also, lights would go on and off at all hours."

That wasn't all. The abundance of supernatural activity in many of the houses suggests that those who built them aren't so willing to let them go. Over the years, more than one family living in these houses has reported seeing shimmering human outlines drifting through the rooms, wandering harmlessly through walls and doors and vanishing from sight when they passed through the exterior walls.

Cornelius goes on to say that some inhabitants would be woken in the middle of the night by the sound of rattling plates and clinking silverware in the kitchen, as though there were someone up doing the dishes. Another common account involved the sound of disembodied footfalls across creaking wooden floorboards. These phantom footsteps would come to life at any time, sometimes stomping across crowded dining rooms in the afternoon, other times waking a household in the middle of the night. In other homes there were the sounds of voices—crying babies, hushed whispers in vacant rooms, sudden shouts coming from empty corners.

According to Cornelius, while the Indian residents were "concerned about these ghosts," it did not take them long to grow accustomed to their spiritual residents. They were all familiar with the history behind the houses; they knew the anguish of the former inhabitants, and acknowledged that such suffering might produce the phenomena so many of them were experiencing. "So," Cornelius says, "Indian families knew they would not be hurt by the ghosts. They just decided to live with them."

Cornelius does not mince words when it comes to explaining the relative ease her people had in accepting the spirits of the Japanese dead. "Being a Nu Wu, I've been very accustomed to seeing things that non-Indians would regard as supernatural. I know that these things exist so I have been raised to be very respectful and just to let them be." There are some families who, in an effort to deal with these sorrowful spirits, run sage smoke through their homes and say prayers for the departed, so that they may rest in peace. Nevertheless, the consensus among Cornelius' people is to accept the spiritual ramifications of the Japanese internment. The events in the Japanese settlements have generally been accepted into the larger spiritual forces that are believed by some to thrive in the surrounding area. "There is a lot of very powerful energy here," Cornelius says. "I know that our medicine people know about these sacred areas and spiritual sites, but we don't talk about these places to anyone. That's just the way it is."

And so the spirits of those relocated Japanese that still haunt their internment camp homes are accepted here in a way they might not be in other parts of the country, where people tend to be far more skittish about such matters. Certainly, though, this is small comfort to those purported spirits, which, even now, are bound to the homes they were forced into over half a century ago.

The Shadow in the Closet

When Andrea Cadiz told this story, she was still living in Phoenix, though she has since moved from Arizona's capital to southern California. "It was a job opportunity that I couldn't say no to," she says today, "but I was glad to leave anyway. All in all, I value the experiences I had in the city. I really enjoyed my time there; I made a good group of friends. Crazy as the heat could get, the people were generally friendly, there was a lot to do and I enjoyed my job. But still, it was time to go." Given the things she experienced during the roughly three months before her latest job offer, one can hardly blame her.

It began when she moved into her new place in the fall of 2003. "It was a two-bedroom condo," she says. "There was more room and I liked the neighborhood better, and the rent was almost the same as what I was paying before. I was really happy about finding it." Andrea chalked the find up to good fortune, a lucky glance at an advertisement in the classifieds. Telling herself that it couldn't hurt to take a look, she ended up taking the place in moments. It was an impulsive decision, she admits, but the rent was unusually low for a condo of that size. She had stumbled on a great deal, and she was not about to let it go, especially given that the lease for her current apartment was just about to expire.

"I moved in a week after I looked at it," she says. "It was a completely normal move. A few friends helped me. We ate pizza on top of the boxes. When everyone left, I didn't feel like there was anything wrong." In other words, there was no hint at the bizarre forces residing within her new living space—bizarre forces that were about to make the next three months the strangest, most unsettling time of her life. And it all began with, of all things, her bedroom closet.

Andrea laughs. "Yeah, I'm sure it's something of a cliché in these ghost stories. A monster in the closet, or else under the bed." In this case, however, there was no actual monster. For Andrea, that first night she noticed it, just the mere sight of the closet was enough to fill her with an inexplicable apprehension—it would not remain inexplicable for long.

"I remember it really clearly," Andrea says. "I'd been reading in bed, and was leaning over to shut off my night-table light when I caught it from the corner of my eye. The closet door was open, and for whatever reason, I got this weird chill when I saw it." When trying to explain, Andrea speaks of how the shadowy opening, dimly illuminated by her bedside light, somehow seemed to exude a presence. "The best way I can explain it, I think, is that the closet didn't *fit*. Right then, I couldn't believe that I'd never noticed it before. You know—had it always been like this? It was like there'd been a guy standing there all along that I hadn't seen until then. It was just a closet, I know, but something about the way it looked was freaking me out."

Wasting no time, Andrea got out of bed and made her way to the closet, trying not to look into its dark interior as she hastily shut the door. Once this was accomplished, she quickly ran back to her bed. "It wasn't nearly as bad with the door closed, but I was still *aware* of it. I remember wondering if I was going crazy, lying there trying to ignore the closet door. I tried to tell myself that I was being ridiculous, but I still couldn't shake the feeling that something really weird was going on."

When she finally fell asleep, it was with her back to the closet, and when she woke up again a few hours later, the closet was the first thing on her mind. "I was wide awake in a second. I still had my back to it, but I could just tell that something was wrong, and all I could think about was that closet. I was picturing it in my head, and it was freaking me right out." Andrea says she didn't want to turn around and look, but knew she was going to anyway. What she saw in the darkness was terrifying, yet somehow inevitable; the closet door was open.

"That was it for me that night," she says. "The jolt I got from that open door, which I *knew* I shut before I went to sleep, was too much." Jumping out of bed with her blankets and her pillow in her arms, Andrea slammed the bedroom door behind her and slept on the living room sofa. So concluded her first bizarre experience in her new place—the first, as it turned out, of a months-long stint of freakish encounters, inside her new home and out.

"I definitely felt off the next morning," she says. "The closet door was still open when I checked on it, but it didn't get to me the way it did the night before. It wasn't the sort of thing I could just forget about, though, and the more I thought about it, the sillier I felt. Really, it was totally possible that I had opened the door in my sleep. I'd never been a sleepwalker growing up, but who knows. Anything's possible, right?"

Whatever the case, Andrea goes on to say that she was determined to put the incident behind her, telling herself that it was absurd, bordering on insane, for an adult to be afraid of a closet. Preoccupied as she was, she didn't give much thought to the strange number of silent phone calls she got at the office that day. Her phone rang four times with no one on the other end. Only later, when this became a regular occurrence, did she think of linking it to the incident in her bedroom.

Things quickly unraveled for Andrea after that. Rational as she was trying to be about it, she could not help but feel uneasy about the closet. While it did not open on its own the night after the initial episode, Andrea was conscious of it as she read in bed, after she turned off the light, and while she was trying to get to sleep. "I had these vivid, really scary dreams about the closet one night," she says. "I can still clearly remember one of them. I was in my bedroom and it was dark and somebody was pushing the door open from the inside. It was dark in the room, but when the door was wide open, it was even darker inside the closet. Then this thing stepped out—not a man, but the outline of a man. He was as black as the closet behind him." Andrea woke then. It was still dark, and as she tried to get back to sleep she avoided looking at the closet, only once glancing sidelong to make sure it was still shut.

"The next day, I was really tired," Andrea says, "and that's the way I stayed for the next three months or so." When she talks about it after the fact, what Andrea stresses most is her disbelief at how long it took her to take matters into her own hands and move out of the place. "It was driving me crazy," she says, "but I was still coming up with all kinds of excuses to avoid getting up and moving again."

It wasn't simple exhaustion that was plaguing her daylight hours. Wherever she went, she couldn't shake the feeling that there was something wrong. Her descriptions of that feeling, vague and convoluted, amount to a sense of a presence, an